D1565273

Spurious Correlations

Spurious Correlations

TYLER VIGEN

NEW YORK   BOSTON

Hachette Books
Hachette Book Group
1290 Avenue of the Americas
New York, NY 10104
HachetteBookGroup.com

Printed in the United States of America

RRD-C

First Edition: May 2015

10   9   8   7   6   5   4   3   2   1

Hachette Books is a division of Hachette Book Group, Inc.
The Hachette Books name and logo are trademarks of Hachette Book Group, Inc.

The publisher is not responsible for websites (or their content) that are not owned by the publisher.

Library of Congress Cataloguing-in-Publication Data

Vigen, Tyler.
Spurious correlations / Tyler Vigen.
pages cm
ISBN 978-0-316-33943-8 (hardback)—ISBN 978-0-316-33945-2 (ebook)   1. American wit and humor.
2. Curiosities and wonders. I. Title.
PN6165. V55 2015
818'.602—dc23
2014049856

Dedicated to Kat—
for supporting all my crazy ideas

Table of Contents

Introduction

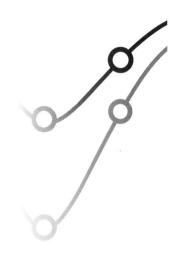

In the late 1800s in Holland, a curious phenomenon occurred: The human birthrate rose at the same pace as the local population of white storks. Generations of parents would later rely on the connection to avoid awkward conversations with their children. While the story faded into folklore, the real-life correlation persisted. New research in the twentieth and twenty-first centuries has consistently confirmed a statistically significant connection between storks and human birthrates in a number of European countries.

In 1958, William Phillips, a professor at the London School of Economics, published a paper regarding the connection between unemployment and inflation. As other economists explored Phillips's data, the correlation spread like wildfire: high inflation rates were linked to low unemployment and vice versa. The policy implications were explicit. National economies needed only to choose between inflation and unemployment, or somehow find a balance between the two. The Phillips curve, as the connection came to be called, informed macroeconomic policy decisions for years in both Europe and the United States.

Humans are biologically inclined to recognize patterns. We spend thousands of dollars on college because education level correlates with monetary earnings later in life. We are attracted to the strong smell of freshly baked cookies because the strength of the aroma correlates with the proximity of the cookies. We go to bed early because a good night's sleep correlates with a better mood the next day. We avoid eating cheese before sleeping because cheese consumption correlates with fatal bedsheet tangling accidents.

Wait, what was that about cheese?

The pattern is clear: a statistical correlation exists between the increasing rate of national cheese consumption and the increasing number of accidental suffocations and strangulations in bed. I've got the graph to prove it:

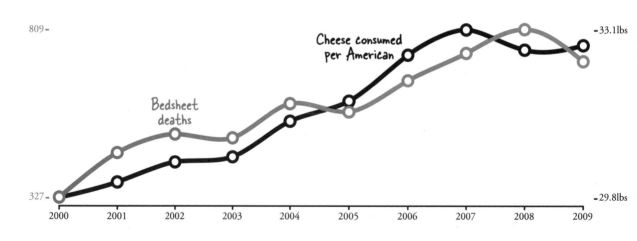

It could be that melted cheese clogs airways. It could be that cheese causes night terrors. Or it could be that the correlation is totally spurious and accountable to chance. Almost certainly it is the latter. Does correlation imply causation? It's intuitive, but it's not always true.

Correlation, as a concept, means strictly that two things vary together. Automobile use correlates with automobile accidents. Warm weather correlates with ice cream sales. Overcast skies correlate with rain. But then there's this one: the number of films Nicolas Cage has appeared in each year correlates with the number of people who have drowned by falling into a swimming pool.

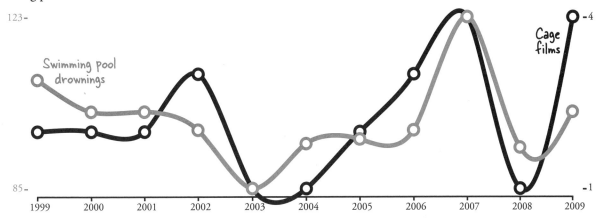

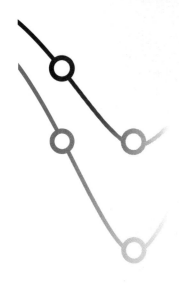

Correlations don't always make sense.

Remember the correlation between babies and storks? It was also coincidence. The modern research into the phenomenon was conducted by scientists who wanted to show that statistics used improperly can provide wildly fallible results, and they succeeded. It turns out William Phillips's theory on economics doesn't hold up either. The inflation-employment connection was pervasive, but it was overly simplistic. Years later, new research showed that Phillips's pattern didn't hold up with long-term data. The variables are related, but they don't directly control each other.

—

Provided enough data, it is possible to find things that correlate even when they shouldn't. The method is often called "data dredging." Data dredging is a technique used to find something that correlates with one variable by comparing it to hundreds of other variables. Normally scientists first hypothesize about a connection between two variables before they analyze data to determine the extent to which that connection exists. For example, testing the theory of whether storks bring babies by correlating storks with birthrates.

Instead of testing individual hypotheses, a computer program can data dredge by simply comparing every dataset to every other dataset. Technology and data collection in the twenty-first century makes this significantly easier. Instead of reading the back of every movie at Blockbuster, I can hop on IMDb.com to find the number of movies Nic Cage appeared in within two minutes. I don't need to track all of Walmart's annual sales to see if there is a correlation to their data; someone at Statista.com has already pulled it from their annual reports. What about deaths from a particular cause? The Centers for Disease Control publishes all its data. How many stay-at-home dads are there? The U.S. Census will give me an estimate. This is the world of big data and big correlations.

—

In the following pages you'll see dozens of correlations between completely unrelated sets of data. Every correlation was discovered by a computer. The correlations were all produced in the same way: One giant database of variables collected from a variety of sources is mined to find unexpected connections.

In order to create each chart, I begin by selecting a statistic I want to correlate. An algorithm then goes through the entire set of statistics and calculates the correlation coefficient for every variable compared to the one I selected. From there the program displays the strongest correlations. In this book I use Pearson's correlation coefficient, which is very common for expressing linear relationships between variables.

Out of the thousands of graphs my algorithm has generated that could have appeared in this book, I had some help selecting which ones would be

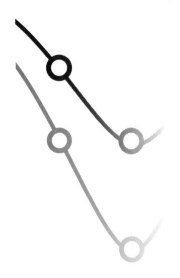

the most fun to show. I sent a link to many of my fellow students here at Harvard Law School and asked them to rate and comment on various graphs. Collectively they cast more than 13,000 votes on how interesting they found each graph, and I wish I had space to thank every one of them by name. Since I don't, maybe I can shift the blame to them instead: If you don't find a particular graph interesting, please blame the students of Harvard Law School.

Despite the humor, this book has a serious side. Graphs can lie, and not all correlations are indicative of an underlying causal connection. Data dredging is part of why it is possible to find so many spurious relationships. The correlations are also strong because very few points are being compared. Instead of comparing just ten years, we should ideally be looking at hundreds of points of comparison. Correlations are an important part of scientific analysis, but they can be misleading if used incorrectly. Even the charts are designed to be subtly deceptive. The data on the Y-axes doesn't always start at zero, which makes the graphs appear to line up much better than they otherwise would. The data points are real and mathematically placed, but they are displayed in a very specific way.

You can double-check any statistic in this book by going to the following web address: http://tylervigen.com/sources. There you will find each data source with a direct link to where the relevant statistic was found. You'll also find plenty more charts not included in this book, many of which have a reduced copyright restriction so that they can be displayed in educational or professional settings as an example of how not to use statistics. This project has been a welcome distraction from law school, to say the least, so I hope you enjoy reading my spurious correlations as much as I enjoyed preparing them for you.

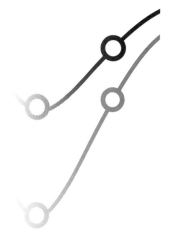

Sources:

R. Murray Thomas, *Blending Qualitative and Quantitative Research Methods in Theses and Dissertations* (Thousand Oaks, CA: Corwin Press, 2003).

Ellen Spector Platt, *Garlic, Onion, and Other Alliums* (Mechanicsburg, PA: Stackpole Books, 2003).

R. Matthews, (2000), Storks Deliver Babies (p= 0.008). *Teaching Statistics*, 22: 36–38.

The Collected Scientific Papers of Paul A. Samuelson

John Phelan, "Milton Friedman and the rise and fall of the Phillips Curve," The Commentator, October 23, 2012. www.thecommentator.com/article/1895/milton_friedman_and_the_rise_and _fall_of_the_phillips_curve

Brian Domitrovic, "The Economics Nobel Goes to Sargent & Sims: Attackers of the Phillips Curve," *Forbes*, October 10, 2011. www.forbes.com/sites/briandomitrovic/2011/10/10/the-economics-nobel -goes-to-sargent-sims-attackers-of-the-phillips-curve

Ingestibles

It's simply a matter of quantity versus quality.

Hot dogs consumed by the men's winner of the Nathan's Hot Dog Eating Contest

vs.

Unique fiction books that made #1 on the New York Times best seller list

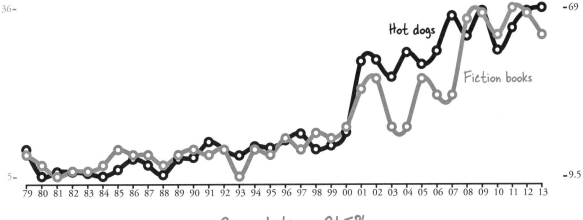

Correlation: 91.5%

You'll notice that the number of hot dogs consumed stays fairly steady up until 2001, where it suddenly jumps. That's the year Takeru Kobayashi realized he could double his hot dog eating rate by eating the hot dog and the bun separately. He calls this the Solomon Method. It has since been improved by the "dunking" method, where competitors dunk the buns in water and wring them out before eating.

SOURCES:
Nathan's Famous Hall of Fame
Hawes Publications, "*New York Times* Best Seller Number Ones Listing Fiction By Date"

Sweet dreams aren't made of cheese. Who am I to dis a Brie?

Cheese consumption

vs.

Fatal bedsheet tangling accidents

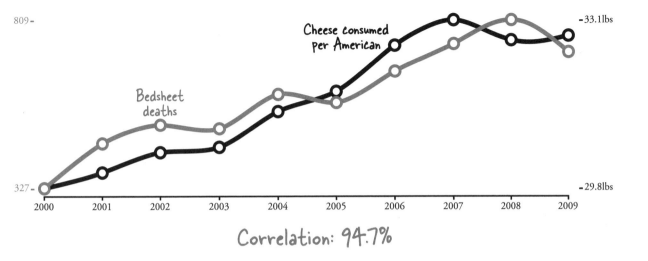

809 -

327 -

- 33.1lbs

- 29.8lbs

Cheese consumed
per American

Bedsheet
deaths

2000 2001 2002 2003 2004 2005 2006 2007 2008 2009

Correlation: 94.7%

The majority of adult humans are lactose intolerant. Thus, it would make more sense to label people who *can* eat dairy. Dairy eaters possess lactase *persistence*, or the lamest superpower ever: the ability to continue consuming dairy into adulthood.

SOURCES:
U.S. Department of Agriculture, Economic Research Service
Centers for Disease Control & Prevention, Detailed Mortality Data
National Institutes of Health, Genetics Home Reference

When "I can't believe it's not butter!" becomes "I can't believe we're still married!"

Margarine consumption

vs.

The divorce rate in Maine

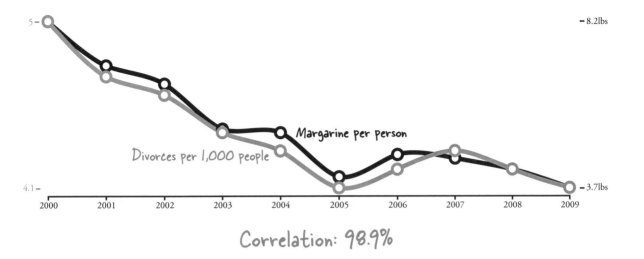

5 —   — 8.2lbs

Margarine per person

Divorces per 1,000 people

4.1 —   — 3.7lbs

2000   2001   2002   2003   2004   2005   2006   2007   2008   2009

Correlation: 98.9%

In 2005, butter was consumed in greater per capita quantities than margarine for the first time since 1957. Yes, this means that from 1957 to 2005, margarine was the leading bread spread. Margarine, in all its synthetic glory, was invented in France in 1869 as a butter alternative for the lower class.

SOURCES:

U.S. Department of Agriculture, Economic Research Service

U.S. National Center for Health Statistics, National Vital Statistics Reports, "Births, Marriages, Divorces, and Deaths: Provisional Data for 2009." (And prior reports. We didn't just extrapolate from 2009 backward.)

The real reason everything tastes like chicken.

Chicken consumption

vs.

Paper and board product consumption

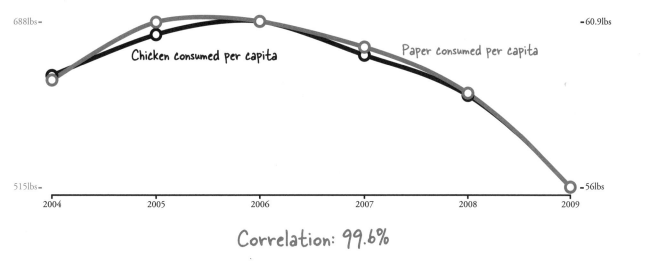

688lbs — Chicken consumed per capita — 60.9lbs

Paper consumed per capita

515lbs — — 56lbs

2004   2005   2006   2007   2008   2009

Correlation: 99.6%

It may appear misleading to equivocate on the word "consumption" here, but it's not. Wood pulp is commonly used as a food additive. It makes a great artificial filler for meat products. And by "great," I mean it has no nutritional value whatsoever.

SOURCES:
U.S. Department of Agriculture, Economic Research Service
U.S. Forest Service, Treesearch and Development (Yes, really.)
NPR: *The Salt*, "From McDonald's To Organic Valley, You're Probably Eating Wood Pulp"

"I'm chokin' it!"

Customer satisfaction with McDonald's

vs.

Deaths caused by obstruction of the respiratory tract following ingestion of food

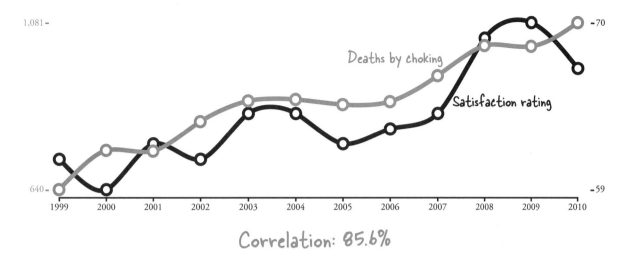

Deaths by choking

Satisfaction rating

Correlation: 85.6%

McDonald's Chicken McNuggets only come in four shapes: the bell, the bow tie, the ball, and the boot.

SOURCES:
American Customer Satisfaction Index, Benchmarks by Industry—Limited-Service Restaurants
Centers for Disease Control & Prevention, Detailed Mortality Data
Business Insider, "Why McDonald's Chicken McNuggets Come In Only Four Shapes"

SURGEON GENERAL'S WARNING: Do not operate light machinery after tea consumption.

Tea consumption

vs.

People killed by misusing a lawnmower

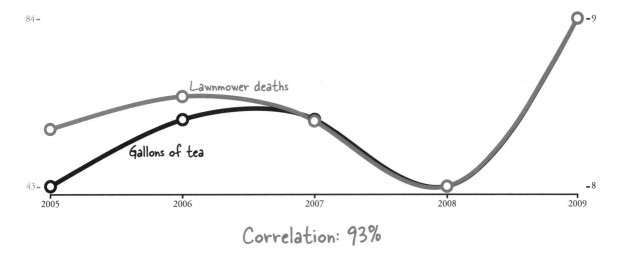

84-
-9

Lawnmower deaths

Gallons of tea

43-
-8
2005   2006   2007   2008   2009

Correlation: 93%

If all the tea dumped into Boston Harbor on December 16, 1773, was distributed equally to U.S. citizens today, we'd each get one tablespoon of tea. If it was distributed to all the citizens of the colonies at the time, they would each have gotten over half a gallon.

SOURCES:

U.S. Department of Agriculture, Economic Research Service

Boston Tea Party Museum (The measurements "one tablespoon" and "half a gallon" are dependent on how strong you like your tea, since the dumped tea was dry tea leaves. In theory, the entire Boston Harbor was briefly the largest, weakest cup of tea in history. These numbers assume that a pound of dry tea leaves makes about 200 cups of tea.)

Centers for Disease Control & Prevention, Detailed Mortality Data

Yet another health benefit of vegetarianism.

Beef consumption

vs.

Deaths caused by lightning

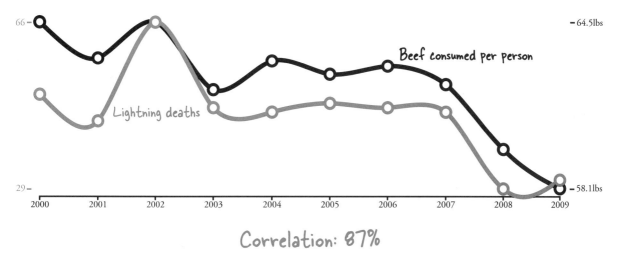

66 –

29 –

2000 2001 2002 2003 2004 2005 2006 2007 2008 2009

Beef consumed per person

Lightning deaths

– 64.5lbs

– 58.1lbs

Correlation: 87%

Men account for over five times as many lightning-related deaths as women.

SOURCES:
U.S. Department of Agriculture, Economic Research Service
Centers for Disease Control & Prevention, Detailed Mortality Data

Bringing new meaning to "natural gas."

Customer satisfaction with Taco Bell

vs.

International oil production

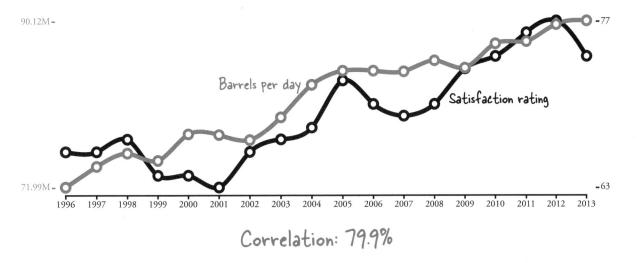

90.12M-

Barrels per day

Satisfaction rating

71.99M-

-77

-63

1996 1997 1998 1999 2000 2001 2002 2003 2004 2005 2006 2007 2008 2009 2010 2011 2012 2013

Correlation: 79.9%

In 2013, the United States overtook Saudi Arabia to become the world's top oil-producing nation. The United States is now responsible for 14 percent of worldwide oil production (and 22 percent of its consumption).

SOURCES:
American Customer Satisfaction Index, Benchmarks by Industry—Limited-Service Restaurants
Energy Information Administration, International Energy Statistics

Garfield makes *everyone* hungry.

Potatoes used for frozen french fries

vs.

Instances of Garfield eating lasagna

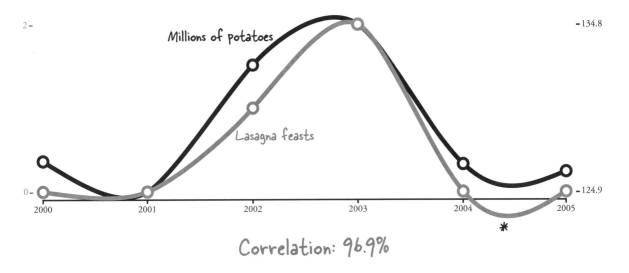

Millions of potatoes

Lasagna feasts

Correlation: 96.9%

Despite his signature love of lasagna, Garfield eats it surprisingly rarely. In 2002, he only ate lasagna once (April 7). Here are some of the other things he ate that year: a moldy brownie, Jon's pet fish, a small woodland creature, and leftover meat loaf.

SOURCES:
U.S. Department of Agriculture, Potatoes Summary
Garfield comic strips (We manually reviewed thousands of *Garfield* strips to get this data: every daily strip from 1978 to the present.)

* This graph displays one of the struggles associated with using Bézier curves to connect linear points. Garfield has decidedly never eaten lasagna fewer than zero times, but this graph implies that he did sometime between 2004 and 2005.

**Customers are only happy with KFC
when they're eating elsewhere.**

Fish consumption

vs.

Customer satisfaction with KFC

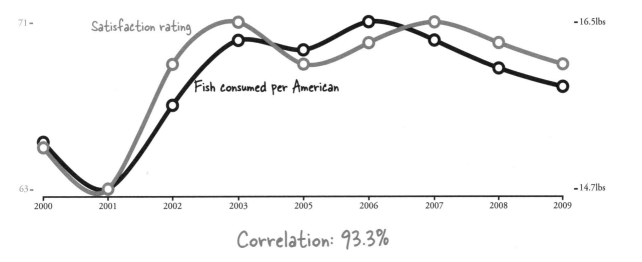

Satisfaction rating

Fish consumed per American

Correlation: 93.3%

The American Customer Satisfaction Index tracks customer satisfaction by polling around 70,000 people per year. In the fast-food department, pizza places consistently score much better than other restaurant types. The top four fast-food chains in terms of customer satisfaction are Pizza Hut, Papa John's, Little Caesars, and Domino's. KFC ranks between Dunkin' Donuts and Taco Bell.

SOURCES:
U.S. Department of Agriculture, Economic Research Service
American Customer Satisfaction Index, Benchmarks by Industry—Limited-Service Restaurants

$timul@te y0ur $oyb3ans.

Use of genetically engineered soybeans

vs.

E—mail spam

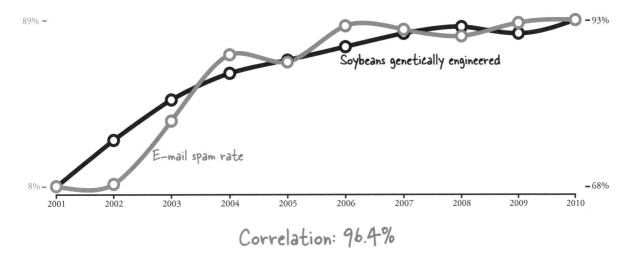

If you received an e-mail while eating soybeans in 2009, there is an 80 percent chance that both the soybeans were genetically modified and the e-mail was spam.

SOURCES:
Emailtray, based on reports from various anti-spam services
U.S. Department of Agriculture, Economic Research Service, "Adoption of Genetically Engineered Crops in the U.S."

McDonald's begins selling the Filet-O-Fish internationally.

McDonald's global revenue

vs.

Value of U.S. exports of non-edible fishery product

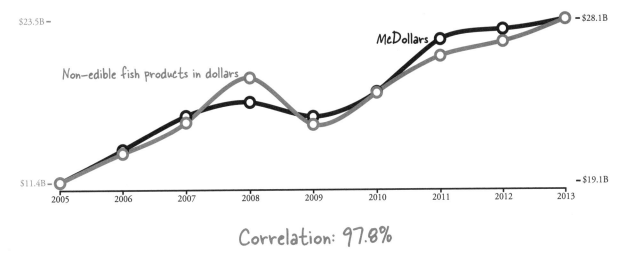

$23.5B — — $28.1B

Non-edible fish products in dollars

McDollars

$11.4B — — $19.1B

2005 2006 2007 2008 2009 2010 2011 2012 2013

Correlation: 97.8%

McDonald's operates in 118 countries, but it doesn't serve the same thing everywhere. In China, you can get McWings—crispy buffalo chicken wings. In India, McDonald's is certified halal and doesn't serve beef or pork. In Malaysia, you can get a cornmeal bun. In Hungary, you can order the McFarm, which is a double cheeseburger made with pork instead of beef and mayonnaise instead of ketchup. In the United States, you can even get breakfast at McDonald's! (McDonald's breakfast hasn't caught on internationally like it has in the States.)

SOURCES:
McDonald's Annual Reports
McDonalds Local Menu Items
U.S. National Oceanic and Atmospheric Administration, "Summary of Imports and Exports of Fishery Products"

Better ingredients, better pizza.

Tree nut consumption

vs.

Customer satisfaction with Domino's Pizza

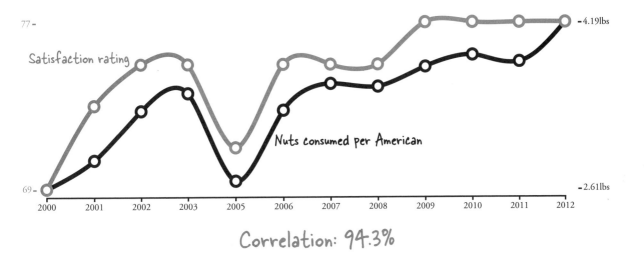

Satisfaction rating

Nuts consumed per American

Correlation: 94.3%

Yes, I know that's Papa John's slogan, not Domino's. In 1998, a third chain, Pizza Hut, sued Papa John's for false advertising over "Better ingredients. Better pizza." The jury initially awarded Pizza Hut almost half a million dollars in damages, but the court of appeals overturned the verdict after Papa John's argued that no one actually relied on "Better ingredients. Better pizza" when deciding which pizza to order.

SOURCES:
U.S. Department of Agriculture, Economic Research Service
American Customer Satisfaction Index, Benchmarks by Industry—Limited-Service Restaurants

Brad Pitt single-handedly drives national
ice cream consumption rates.

Ice cream consumption

vs.

Brad Pitt's earnings

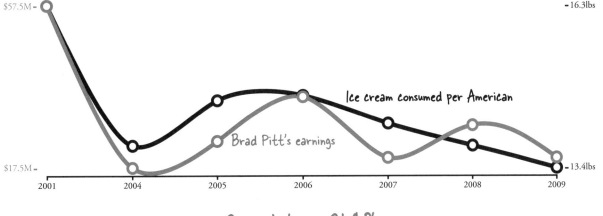

$57.5M -

$17.5M -

2001   2004   2005   2006   2007   2008   2009

- 16.3lbs

Ice cream consumed per American

Brad Pitt's earnings

- 13.4lbs

Correlation: 91.4%

I would be remiss not to mention one of the most commonly cited correlations: ice cream consumption with murder rates. The seasonal correlation is incredibly strong. Murders are significantly more common in the summer than in the winter. The connection between ice cream and murder is, of course, spurious.

SOURCES:
U.S. Department of Agriculture, Economic Research Service
The Richest: Brad Pitt Net Worth

Revenge of the shrimp.

U.S. supply of shrimp

vs.

People killed by sharp glass

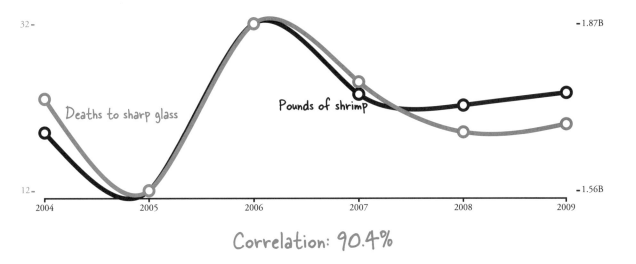

32-

-1.87B

Deaths to sharp glass

Pounds of shrimp

12-

-1.56B

2004   2005   2006   2007   2008   2009

Correlation: 90.4%

How much does the head of a shrimp weigh? I thought you'd never ask. Surprisingly, it depends on where it originates. Shrimp heads account for 43 percent of the total weight from shrimp harvested off New England or the Pacific Ocean, but only 37.1 percent of those caught in the south Atlantic or the Gulf of Mexico. Further proof that Californians and New Englanders are big-headed.

SOURCES:
U.S. National Oceanic and Atmospheric Administration, Office of Science and Technology: Fisheries of the United States (Head-off weight.)
Centers for Disease Control & Prevention, Detailed Mortality Data

Canadians exhale tuna fish.

Total supply of canned tuna in the United States

vs.

Canada's carbon dioxide emissions

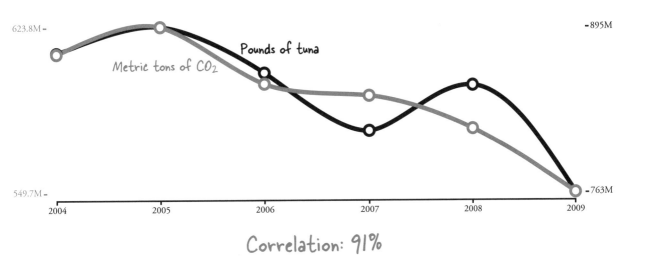

623.8M –

895M

Pounds of tuna

Metric tons of CO_2

549.7M –

763M

| 2004 | 2005 | 2006 | 2007 | 2008 | 2009 |

Correlation: 91%

My research failed to determine why it is natural to say "tuna fish" but strange to say "turkey bird."

SOURCES:
U.S. National Oceanic and Atmospheric Administration, National Marine Fisheries Service, "Fisheries of the United States"
U.S. Energy Information Administration

Please be kind, rewind, and don't touch
the tape with your greasy fingers.

Consumption of fats and oils

vs.

Households that still have a VCR

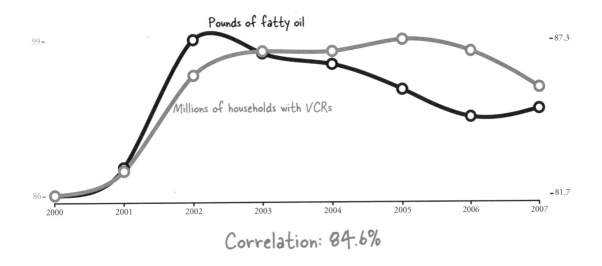

Pounds of fatty oil

Millions of households with VCRs

99–   –87.3

86–   –81.7

2000   2001   2002   2003   2004   2005   2006   2007

Correlation: 84.6%

The FDA definition of fats and oils includes butter, margarine, and cooking oil. It also includes edible beef tallow, which is solid at room temperature and is used in shortening and french fries. Yum.

SOURCES:
U.S. Department of Agriculture, Economic Research Service
Television Bureau of Advertising, Inc., "Trends in Television"

Real hipsters drank 2 percent milk before it got cool.

2 percent milk consumption

vs.

Vinyl LP sales

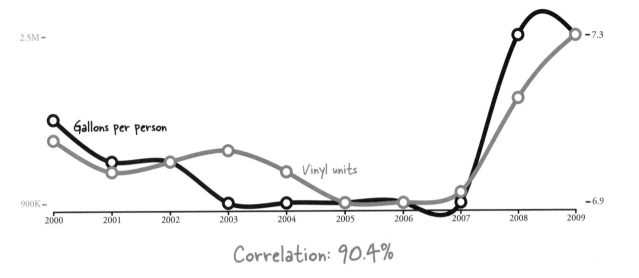

Per capita consumption of whole milk

correlates with

Vinyl album sales

Correlation: 90.4%

Ever wonder why we have 1 and 2 percent milk but we don't have 3 or 4 percent? It's because unaltered whole milk is naturally only about 3.5 percent milkfat.

SOURCES:
Nielsen SoundScan
U.S. Department of Agriculture, Economic Research Service

Science 'n' Shit

Freshman move-in day is more dangerous than you thought.

Undergraduate enrollment at U.S. universities

vs.

Injuries related to falling TVs

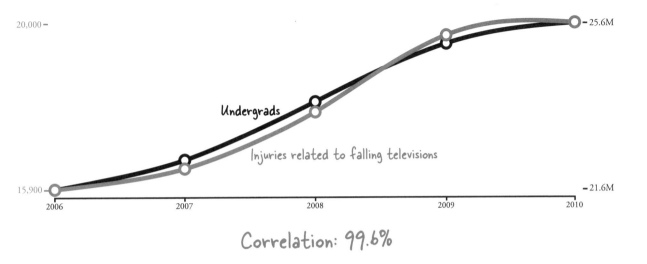

20,000 —

Undergrads

Injuries related to falling televisions

15,900 —
2006   2007   2008   2009   2010

— 25.6M

— 21.6M

Correlation: 99.6%

Unsurprisingly, injuries related to falling televisions have an even stronger correlation to television sales. That graph does not appear in this book, but look for it in my upcoming sequel: *Not-So-Spurious Correlations*.

SOURCES:
College Board, "Trends in Student Aid"
U.S. Consumer Product Safety Commission, "Instability of televisions, furniture, and appliances: Estimated injuries and reported fatalities."

On second thought, this might not be spurious.

Computer science doctorates

vs.

Comic book sales

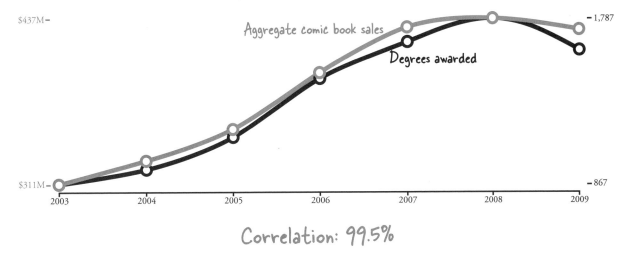

$437M –
$311M –

Aggregate comic book sales

Degrees awarded

– 1,787

– 867

2003   2004   2005   2006   2007   2008   2009

Correlation: 99.5%

Comic book sales numbers are limited to comics delivered to comic book stores by Diamond Comic Distributors. While this is only one company, Diamond completely dominates the comic book distribution industry to such an extent that computing the effects of its competitors is unnecessary.

SOURCES:
National Science Foundation, "Numbers of Doctorates Awarded Continue to Grow in 2009; Indicators of Employment Outcomes Mixed"
Comichron, "Comic Book Sales by Year"

Are recent bee disappearances linked to a secret NATO resolution?

Honey-producing bee colonies in the United States

vs.

Nuclear weapons in Russia's stockpile

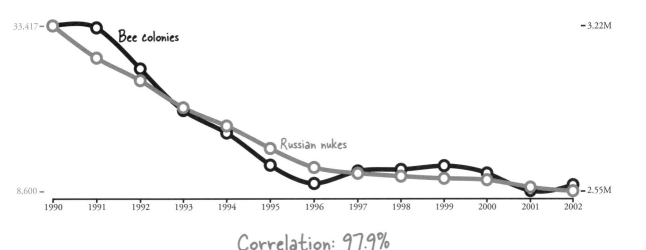

33,417 —

Bee colonies

Russian nukes

8,600 —

1990 1991 1992 1993 1994 1995 1996 1997 1998 1999 2000 2001 2002

— 3.22M

— 2.55M

Correlation: 97.9%

Worker bees only live for about six weeks during peak honey-producing months. In their short lifetime, each bee produces about ½ teaspoon of honey. Thus, the honey required to fill your 12-ounce honey bear was the complete life work of more than eight hundred bees.

SOURCES:
National Resources Defense Council, "Global Nuclear Weapons Stockpiles, 1945–2002"
U.S. Department of Agriculture, National Agricultural Statistics Service: Honey
National Honey Board

Have you seen the new documentary, *Sharknado*?

Shark attacks

vs.

Tornadoes

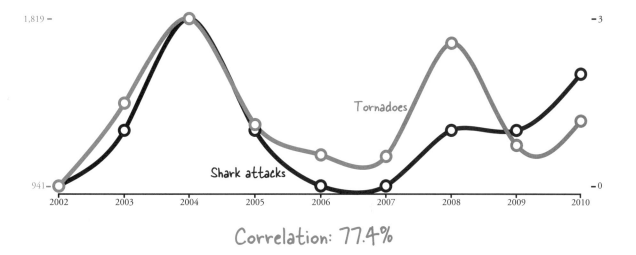

1,819 –

941 –

– 3

– 0

2002 2003 2004 2005 2006 2007 2008 2009 2010

Tornadoes

Shark attacks

Correlation: 77.4%

According to a scientist at the National Severe Storms Laboratory, a tornado would most likely fillet a shark. On a related note, this would be the first entry in my new idea for a cookbook: *Statistically Unlikely Recipes*.

SOURCES:

Florida Museum of Natural History, "International Shark Attack File"

Wikipedia: "List of fatal, unprovoked shark attacks in the United States" (Wikipedia editors attribute more deaths to shark attacks than official reports do. Those cases considered "unconfirmed" are included in the chart.)

U.S. National Weather Service

Mother Jones, "Can a 'Sharknado' Really Happen?"

Inappropriate application of string theory.

Federal funding for science, space, and technology

vs.

Suicides by hanging, strangulation, and suffocation

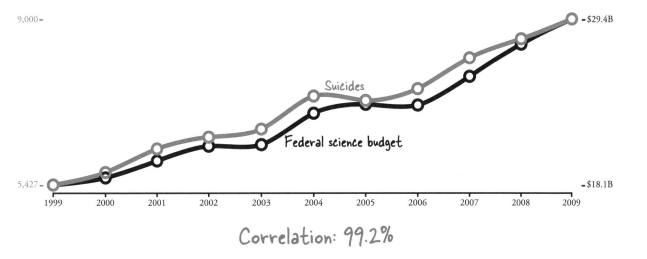

9,000 –

– $29.4B

Suicides

Federal science budget

5,427 –

– $18.1B

1999 2000 2001 2002 2003 2004 2005 2006 2007 2008 2009

Correlation: 99.2%

As of 2008, the nation's R&D fund dedicates 15.3 percent of its budget to defense and just 1.4 percent to space. However, an unspecified portion of the defense R&D includes "space-related defense activities." I hope this includes a starfleet we don't know about yet.

SOURCES:
U.S. Office of Management and Budget, Science & Technology Expenditures
Centers for Disease Control & Prevention, Detailed Mortality Data

A-R-A-C-H-N-O-P-H-O-B-I-A.

Letters in the winning word in the
Scripps National Spelling Bee

vs.

Deaths due to venomous spiders

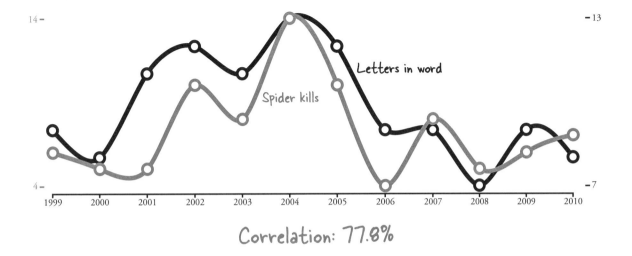

14 –   – 13

Letters in word

Spider kills

4 –   – 7
1999   2000   2001   2002   2003   2004   2005   2006   2007   2008   2009   2010

Correlation: 77.8%

The difficulty rating of words in the Scripps National Spelling Bee is based on a very complicated mathematical algorithm involving a linguistical analysis of the origin of the word, the syllables, and expected phonetic construction.

Just kidding. A couple of wordsmiths sit around a table and throw out difficulty ratings like they're judging a swan dive.

SOURCES:
Scripps National Spelling Bee (We counted the letters.)
Centers for Disease Control & Prevention, Detailed Mortality Data

Law students take to reading while biking to school.

Law books published

vs.

Bicyclists killed in collision with stationary object

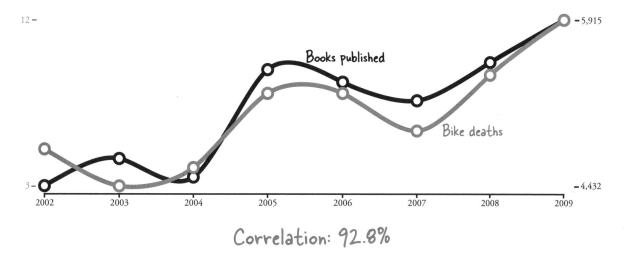

Correlation: 92.8%

Law professors prepare casebooks, which consist primarily of abridged legal opinions that anyone can access but that students are required to purchase for hundreds of dollars. These books don't bother to summarize the law, though, so law students have taken to summarizing classes in course outlines they share with each succeeding generation of law students. These "outlines" can be two to three hundred pages in length. Thus, law professors have outsourced the practice of authoring actual textbooks to judges and students but are still the ones earning royalties.

SOURCES:
Bowker, New Book Titles and Editions
Centers for Disease Control & Prevention, Detailed Mortality Data

What exactly are they serving in school cafeterias?

Biology and biomedical doctorates awarded

vs.

Value of all food sold in grade schools

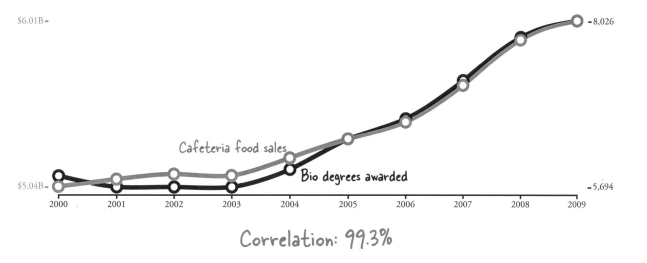

$6.01B —   — 8,026

Cafeteria food sales

$5.04B —   — 5,694
2000   2001   2002   2003   2004   2005   2006   2007   2008   2009

Bio degrees awarded

Correlation: 99.3%

Cafeteria sales are still dwarfed by food sold at gas stations. In 2008, Americans spent more than nine billion dollars on yesterday's roller dogs and stale doughnuts.

SOURCES:
National Science Foundation, "Numbers of Doctorates Awarded Continue to Grow in 2009; Indicators of Employment Outcomes Mixed"
National Restaurant Association, "Restaurant Numbers: 25 Year History, 1970–1995"

Civil engineers choose string cheese over string theory.

Civil engineering doctorates

vs.

Mozzarella cheese consumption

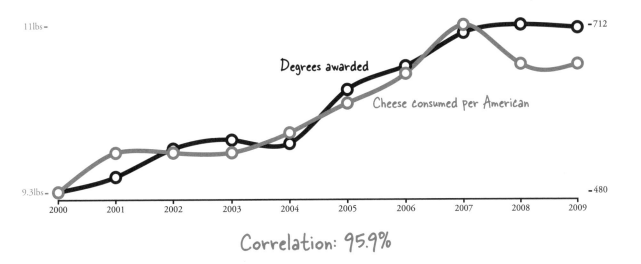

11lbs –   – 712

Degrees awarded

Cheese consumed per American

9.3lbs –   – 480
    2000   2001   2002   2003   2004   2005   2006   2007   2008   2009

Correlation: 95.9%

We will officially be in "the future" when civil engineers need to factor string theory into their plans.

SOURCES:
National Science Foundation, "Numbers of Doctorates Awarded Continue to Grow in 2009; Indicators of Employment Outcomes Mixed"
U.S. Department of Agriculture, Economic Research Service

Those who can't do, teach. Those who can't teach become lawyers. Those lawyers who end up in Washington State write about philosophy.

Philosophy books published

vs.

Lawyers in Washington State

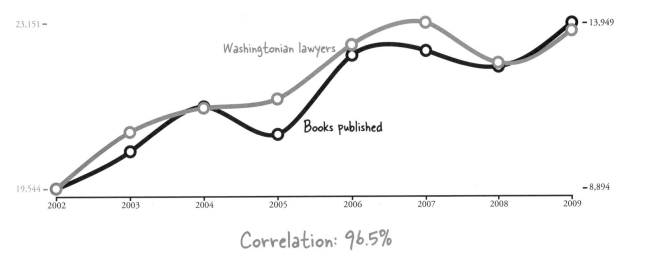

23,151 –

Washingtonian lawyers

– 13,949

Books published

19,544 –

– 8,894

2002   2003   2004   2005   2006   2007   2008   2009

Correlation: 96.5%

Bowker takes a freewheeling approach to classifying books as "philosophy." You might be thinking about Aristotle and Plato. Bowker is thinking about Webster and Britannica. Their "philosophy" category includes dictionaries, encyclopedias, yearbooks, handbooks, bibliographies, and databases.

Sources:
Bowker, New Book Titles and Editions
American Bar Association, "National Lawyer Population by State"

New sociology PhDs realize there is no work in their field, take jobs as astronauts instead.

Sociology doctorates

vs.

Worldwide noncommercial space launches

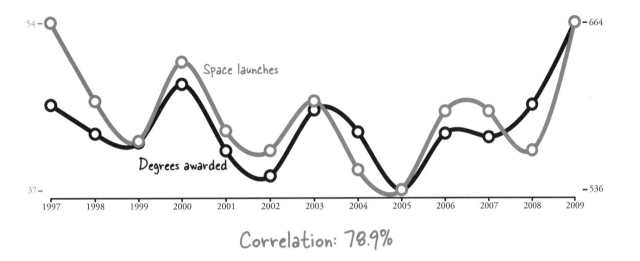

Correlation: 78.9%

Sociologists may simply be discovering the Fermi Paradox. The Fermi Paradox (simplified) says that if there is extraterrestrial life out there, we should have met it by now. If there is no extraterrestrial life, we shouldn't exist.

Sources:
National Science Foundation, "Numbers of Doctorates Awarded Continue to Grow in 2009; Indicators of Employment Outcomes Mixed"
Federal Aviation Administration, Commercial Space Transportation: "2010 Year in Review"
SETI Institute, "Fermi Paradox"

Save the planet! Knock down the old bridges!

Ozone near ground level

vs.

Functionally obsolete bridges

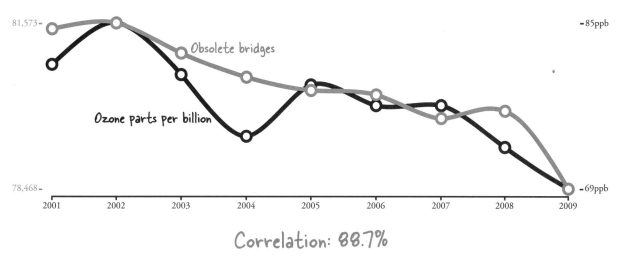

81,573 -
78,468 -

Obsolete bridges

Ozone parts per billion

85ppb
69ppb

2001 2002 2003 2004 2005 2006 2007 2008 2009

Correlation: 88.7%

Ozone is a finicky thing. We want more of it in the stratosphere where it protects us from solar radiation, but we want less of it at ground level where it leads to lung damage.

SOURCES:
U.S. Environmental Protection Agency (Parts per billion is just a way of removing some of the decimal places from parts per million.)
U.S. Federal Highway Administration, Office of Bridge Technology

Herbs. Not even once.

Herb gardening rate

vs.

Bankruptcy

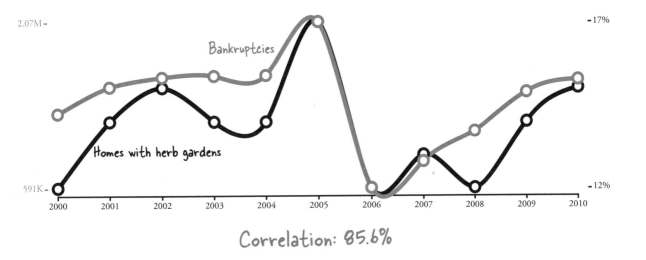

Bankruptcies

2.07M

Homes with herb gardens

591K

17%

12%

2000 2001 2002 2003 2004 2005 2006 2007 2008 2009 2010

Correlation: 85.6%

The drop of bankruptcies in 2006 is due to the Bankruptcy Abuse Prevention and Consumer Protection Act of 2005, which made it tougher to file for bankruptcy. In fact, that also accounts for the spike in bankruptcies in 2005, as people rushed to file before the act was passed.

Sources:
The National Gardening Association, National Gardening Survey (2,000 respondents)
Credit Slips, Bob Lawless, "Bankruptcies Down 12% in 2014, Forecast Predicts the Same Decline for 2015"

Smoke breaks were the only reason to have a pretty view outside.

Homes with landscaping

vs.

Adults who smoke cigarettes

Correlation: 93.2%

In the late 1990s and early 2000s, a greater percentage of high school students smoked than adults. Since 2009, however, adults have once again taken the lead.

SOURCES:
The National Gardening Association, National Gardening Survey (2,000 respondents)
Centers for Disease Control & Prevention, Smoking & Tobacco Use

Political science PhDs are always acting.

Political science doctorates

vs.

The biggest movie budget

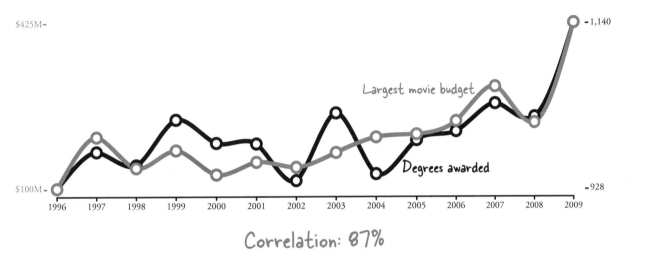

$425M—
$100M—

1996 1997 1998 1999 2000 2001 2002 2003 2004 2005 2006 2007 2008 2009

Largest movie budget

Degrees awarded

—1,140

—928

Correlation: 87%

It costs about $7.5 million per day to keep someone on the International Space Station. *Gravity*'s budget was $110 million. For the same price, Warner Bros. could have actually put Sandra Bullock in the ISS for two weeks.

SOURCES:
National Science Foundation, "Numbers of Doctorates Awarded Continue to Grow in 2009; Indicators of Employment Outcomes Mixed"
The Numbers, Movie Budget and Financial Performance Records

Nothing motivates like Taco Day at the cafeteria!

Public high school enrollment

vs.

Sour cream consumption

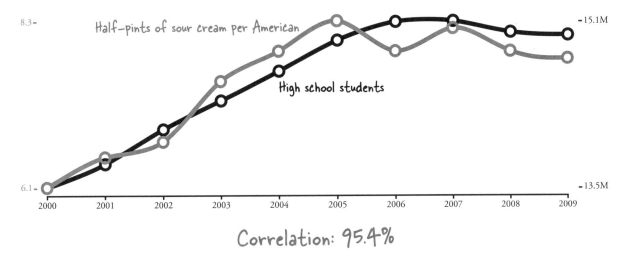

Half-pints of sour cream per American

High school students

Correlation: 95.4%

If there were a list of food items that you should enjoy without understanding how they are made, sour cream would definitely be on it. But since I brought it up, I'll tell you: The fatty layer is separated from un-homogenized cow milk, and bacteria is allowed to ferment and produce lactic acid within the cream, "souring" the cream and producing that tasty white burrito additive.

SOURCES:
National Center for Education Statistics
U.S. Department of Agriculture, Economic Research Service

I knew that's how they spent their time at MIT!

Mechanical engineering doctorates awarded

vs.

World of Warcraft subscribers

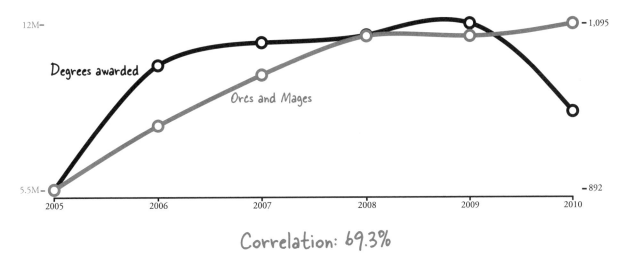

Degrees awarded

Orcs and Mages

12M—

5.5M—

- 1,095

- 892

2005 2006 2007 2008 2009 2010

Correlation: 69.3%

Despite World of Warcraft's reputation as the ubiquitous computer game, it was overtaken in early 2014 by Minecraft. Minecraft has sold over 18 million copies and, at the time of this writing, is the most purchased PC game of all time.

SOURCES:
National Science Foundation, "Numbers of Doctorates Awarded Continue to Grow in 2009; Indicators of Employment Outcomes Mixed"
Activision Blizzard Annual Reports
Mojang, Minecraft Statistics

The Celtics could use a few more hurricanes
to fill out their team this year.

Atlantic hurricanes

vs.

Draft picks by the Boston Celtics

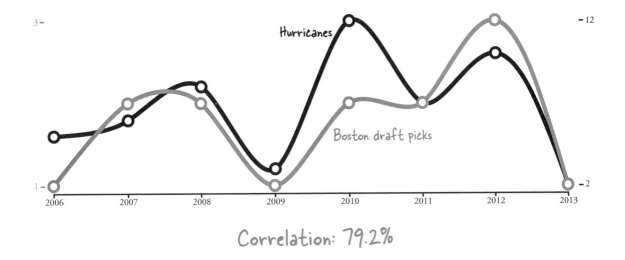

Correlation: 79.2%

The United States began naming Atlantic hurricanes in 1950. For the first few years they used the phonetic alphabet. Starting in 1953, they used strictly female names. It wasn't until 1979, after the responsibility for naming tropical storms was passed off to the UN, that male names were used to describe hurricanes.

SOURCES:
National Weather Service, National Hurricane Center
Basketball-Reference.com: "Boston Celtics Draft Picks"

More than just man's best friend?

Points Harvard's football team scored against Yale

vs.

Valentine's Day spending on pet gifts

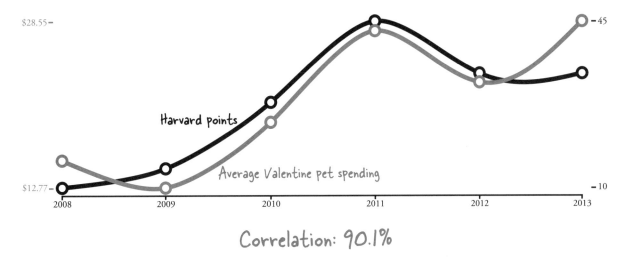

$28.55 —

Harvard points

Average Valentine pet spending

$12.77 —

| 2008 | 2009 | 2010 | 2011 | 2012 | 2013 |

— 45

— 10

Correlation: 90.1%

2014 was a record low year for Valentine's celebrations, with only 53.8 percent of those surveyed reporting that they would be celebrating. That might explain the increase in spending on pets.

SOURCES:
Wikipedia: "List of Harvard-Yale football games"
National Retail Federation, survey question: "How much money do you plan to spend on Valentine's Day gifts for pets?" (6,417 respondents)

It's a good thing you're learning about statistics from this book instead.

High school AP statistics tests taken by males

vs.

Chlamydia rate among males

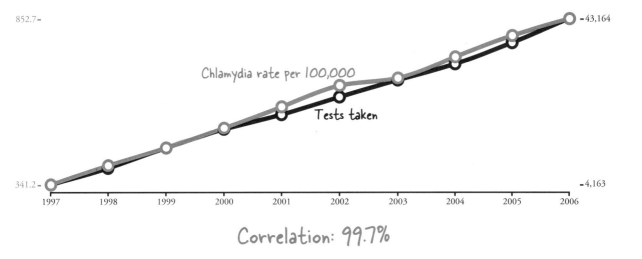

852.7 –
341.2 –

1997 1998 1999 2000 2001 2002 2003 2004 2005 2006

Chlamydia rate per 100,000

Tests taken

– 43,164
– 4,163

Correlation: 99.7%

The AP test with the highest average score is the Chinese language exam, where 68.5 percent of test takers score a perfect 5. Either Chinese is an easy language to learn, or there is some selection bias regarding who decides to take that test.

SOURCES:
College Board
Centers for Disease Control & Prevention, chlamydia rate among males aged 20–24 (Indeed, males aged 20–24 probably aren't taking AP stats tests. That kinda ruins the connection, doesn't it? That's what you get for reading the footnote.)

Cultural Curiosities

Let it go. Let it go. Don't need a job anymore!

Stay-at-home dads

vs.

Walt Disney Company revenue

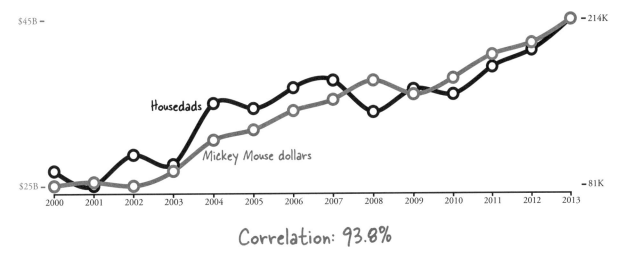

Correlation: 93.8%

In the United States, stay-at-home dads have met the following criteria: Their household contains kids, they haven't had a job (full-time or part-time) for *any* of the past fifty-two weeks, and their spouse has had a job *consistently* for the past fifty-two weeks. If you think this definition is under inclusive, you're not alone. The Bureau of Labor Statistics uses a definition that estimates the same number to be 5 to 10 times larger.

SOURCES:
National At-Home Dad Network
U.S. Census Bureau, Current Population Survey, Annual Social and Economic Supplements
Walt Disney Annual Reports

I've got chills—they're multiplying.

Pregnancy rate

vs.

Power generated by nuclear power plants

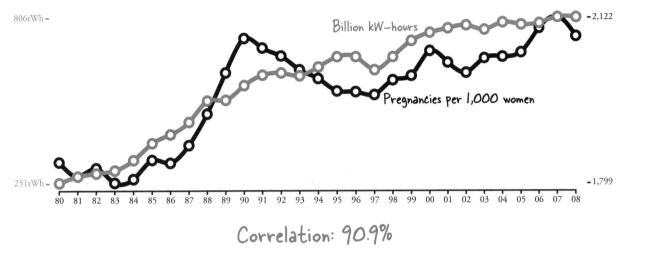

806tWh —
251tWh —

Billion kW-hours

Pregnancies per 1,000 women

— 2,122
— 1,799

80 81 82 83 84 85 86 87 88 89 90 91 92 93 94 95 96 97 98 99 00 01 02 03 04 05 06 07 08

Correlation: 90.9%

The average nuclear power plant in the United States puts out 11.8 billion kilowatt-hours per year, or a ballpark generating capacity of 2 gigawatts. If we toast bread for three minutes in an 800-watt two-slot toaster, this means the average nuclear power plant has an output of about 50 million TPH (toast per hour).

SOURCES:
U.S. National Center for Health Statistics, National Vital Statistics Report: "Births: Final Data for 2008"
Energy Information Administration, Electricity Net Generation (tWh is "terawatt-hours," which is a deviation from the standard "billion kilowatt-hours" generally used for major utility output.)

If you're giving your dog beer,
you're doing Friday night wrong.

Money spent on pets

vs.

Alcohol sold in liquor stores

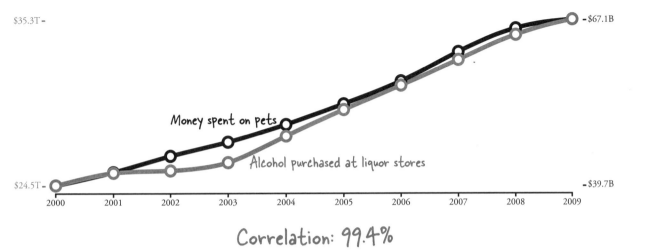

$35.3T$ —
$24.5T$ —

Money spent on pets

Alcohol purchased at liquor stores

— $67.1B
— $39.7B

2000 2001 2002 2003 2004 2005 2006 2007 2008 2009

Correlation: 99.4%

In 2008, everything dropped—from the housing market to life insurance policy purchases. Spending on dogs and beer, however, didn't budge. What's more, that "T" in alcohol spending is for "trillion." In 2009, Americans spent ten times the value of the national debt on alcohol.

SOURCES:
U.S. Department of Agriculture, Economic Research Service
U.S. Bureau of Economic Analysis, "Survey of Current Business"

Do-it-yourself baptisms are not a safe alternative.

Books published about religion

vs.

Bathtub drownings

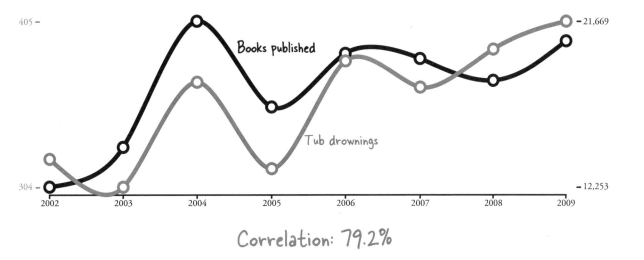

405 —
304 —

2002 2003 2004 2005 2006 2007 2008 2009

Books published

Tub drownings

— 21,669
— 12,253

Correlation: 79.2%

The output of published books about religion is steadily increasing, unlike the publishing of books about computers. Since the dot-com boom, computer book publishing numbers have plateaued.

Sources:
Bowker, New Book Titles and Editions
Centers for Disease Control & Prevention, Detailed Mortality Data

Talk about a *captive* audience.

Days of Our Lives viewership

vs.

Death row inmates

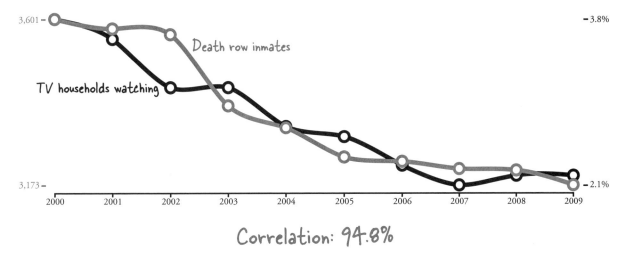

3,601 — — 3.8%

Death row inmates

TV households watching

3,173 — — 2.1%

2000 2001 2002 2003 2004 2005 2006 2007 2008 2009

Correlation: 94.8%

The number of TV shows viewers can watch is growing substantially faster than the number of TV viewers. No series is likely to come close to matching the viewership of the *M*A*S*H* series finale in 1983, which garnered more than 105 million viewers, and certainly no show will ever match the record 67.3 Nielsen rating set by *I Love Lucy* in 1953.

SOURCES:
Nielsen Media Research
U.S. Department of Justice Bureau of Justice Statistics, "Capital Punishment"

Famous last word.

Deaths caused by cataclysmic storm

vs.

Greatest number of f*cks in a movie

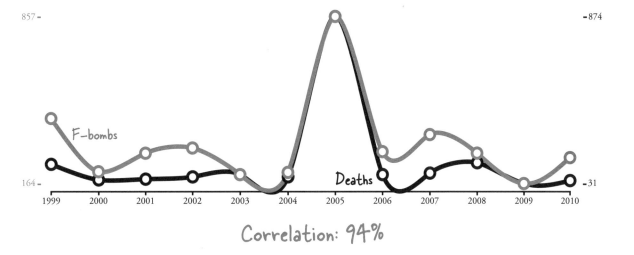

857 –   – 874

F-bombs

164 –   Deaths   – 31

1999 2000 2001 2002 2003 2004 2005 2006 2007 2008 2009 2010

Correlation: 94%

Death counts from major storms and floods often end up artificially inflated because the storms exacerbate preexisting medical conditions. Researchers have difficulty dealing with this anomaly since the deaths are often still *caused* by the storm. After a major storm, the normal death rate in the area decreases for a few days as some of the individuals who would have died a little later instead died during the storm.

SOURCES:

Centers for Disease Control & Prevention, Detailed Mortality Data

Junko Otani, *Older People in Natural Disasters: The Great Hanshin Earthquake of 1995*

Wikipedia: "List of films that most frequently use the word 'fuck'" (You didn't think I was going to use it, did you? You thought I was going to stand behind that asterisk and wimp out of swearing in the citation. Nope.)

D.A.R.E. to resist the symphony.

Gross revenue from U.S. symphony orchestras

vs.

Juvenile arrests for pot possession

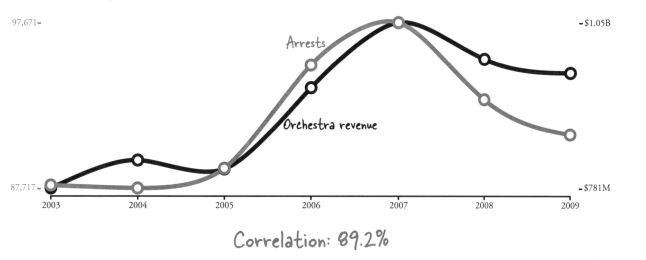

97,671 —

Arrests

Orchestra revenue

87,717 —

— $1.05B

— $781M

2003　2004　2005　2006　2007　2008　2009

Correlation: 89.2%

There was a marked spike in marijuana arrests in 2007, but the violent crime rate was still lower than any year in the 1990s.

SOURCES:
League of American Orchestras, "New York, NY, Performing Arts—Selected Data: 1990 to 2009"
U.S. Department of Justice Uniform Crime Reports

Kentuckians ought to seriously consider more traditional marriage venues.

The marriage rate in Kentucky

vs.

People who drowned after falling out of a fishing boat

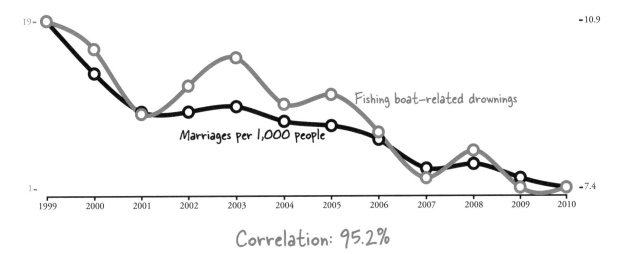

Fishing boat-related drownings

Marriages per 1,000 people

19- ·10.9

1- ·7.4

1999 2000 2001 2002 2003 2004 2005 2006 2007 2008 2009 2010

Correlation: 95.2%

Nevada has the highest marriage rate of any U.S. state by a huge margin. In 1990, Nevada's marriage rate was 99 marriages per 1,000 people, while the next highest state was sitting at 15. The confounding variable is, of course, Las Vegas.

SOURCES:
CDC/NCHS, National Vital Statistics System, "Marriages and Divorces"
Centers for Disease Control & Prevention, Detailed Mortality Data

Why else would you build a bridge, except
so that you could go buy alcohol?

Alcohol sold in grocery stores

vs.

Total number of bridges in the United States

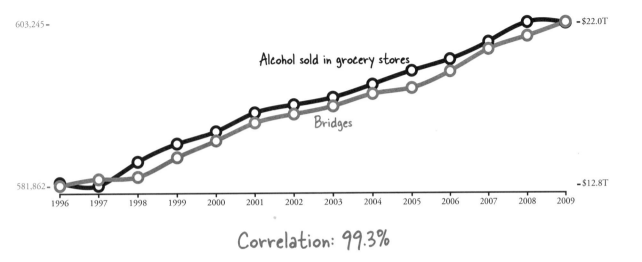

603,245 –

Alcohol sold in grocery stores

Bridges

581,862 –

– $22.0T

– $12.8T

1996 1997 1998 1999 2000 2001 2002 2003 2004 2005 2006 2007 2008 2009

Correlation: 99.3%

As of 2010, the United States had 18,780 miles of bridges, with an average bridge length of approximately 50 meters. Thus, we've built enough bridges to get about 8 percent of the way to the moon.

SOURCES:
U.S. Department of Agriculture, Economic Research Service
U.S. Federal Highway Administration, Office of Bridge Technology
Space.com, "How far is the moon?" (Answer: Very far.)

To do: Research Tolstoy's influence on suicides by passenger train.

Literature books published

vs.

Suicides by hanging

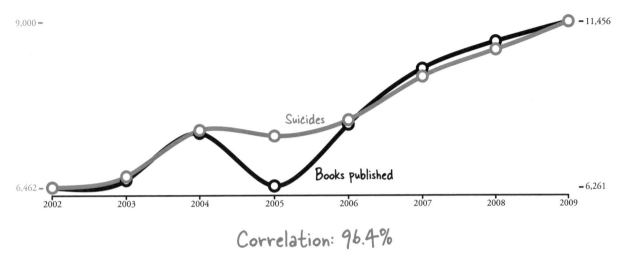

Correlation: 96.4%

In the United States, hanging is not the most popular method of suicide. Number 1 is a category of large firearms. Number 2 is handguns. Number 3 is hanging. Number 4 is a separate category of large firearms. We sure do love our guns.

SOURCES:
Bowker, New Book Titles and Editions
Centers for Disease Control & Prevention, Detailed Mortality Data

Bazinga, Argentina!

The Big Bang Theory viewership

vs.

Percentage of Argentina's GDP spent by the government

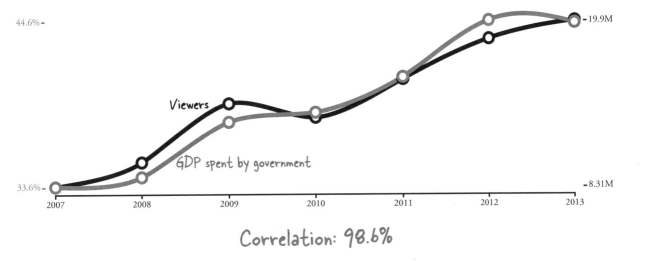

44.6% –

Viewers

GDP spent by government

33.6% –
2007　　2008　　2009　　2010　　2011　　2012　　2013

– 19.9M

– 8.31M

Correlation: 98.6%

The *Euglossa bazinga* is a species of bee in Argentina. That's not spurious: The bee was named after Sheldon's favorite word.

SOURCES:
Wikipedia: "The Big Bang Theory"
Smithsonian Magazine, "A Brand New Bee Was Just Named After Sheldon From *The Big Bang Theory*"
International Monetary Fund, World Economic Outlook Database

They made me list this as "spurious."

Reports of UFOs shaped like discs

vs.

Adults under correctional supervision
in the United States

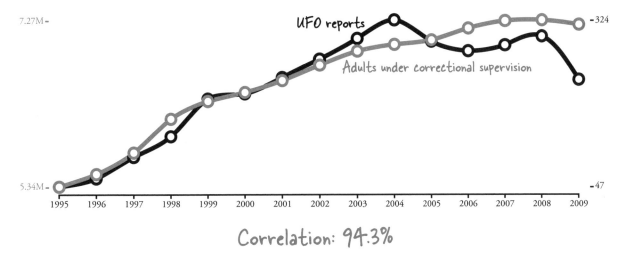

UFO reports

Adults under correctional supervision

7.27M-

5.34M-

1995 1996 1997 1998 1999 2000 2001 2002 2003 2004 2005 2006 2007 2008 2009

-324

-47

Correlation: 94.3%

About 3.1 percent of all adults in the United States are under correctional supervision. Most of these people are on probation, not in prison.

SOURCES:
National UFO Reporting Center
U.S. Department of Justice, Bureau of Justice Statistics

The NBA needs to stop projecting its
flaming basketballs into the sky.

March Madness TV ad revenue

vs.

Reports of flying fireballs

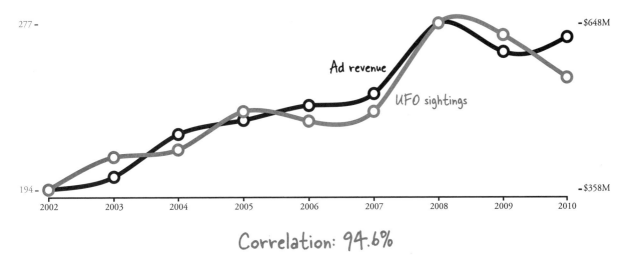

277 –
194 –

2002　2003　2004　2005　2006　2007　2008　2009　2010

Ad revenue

UFO sightings

– $648M
– $358M

Correlation: 94.6%

2008 was the first year that the top seeds became the Final Four. That is, the teams that everyone thought were going to win, won. This also means that prior to 2008, the NCAA tournament selection committee was wrong *every year* in predicting the best teams.

SOURCES:
Kantar Media
National UFO Reporting Center

Aliens are cougars.

Age of the *American Idol* winner

vs.

UFO sightings in New Hampshire

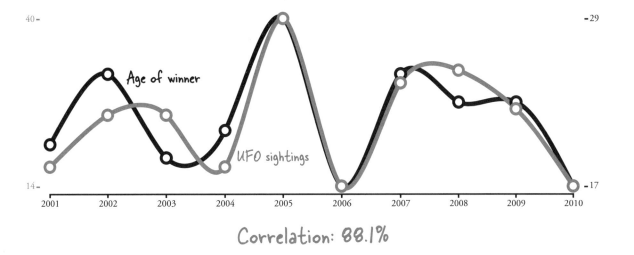

40 —   — 29

Age of winner

UFO sightings

14 —   — 17
2001   2002   2003   2004   2005   2006   2007   2008   2009   2010

Correlation: 88.1%

More UFOs are spotted between the hours of nine p.m. and eleven p.m. than during all daylight hours combined. Those aliens sure are a shy bunch.

SOURCES:
Wikipedia: "List of *American Idol* finalists"
National UFO Reporting Center

A ltr 4 u.

U.S. citizens who are able to receive a text message

vs.

Price to send a letter via the U.S. Postal Service

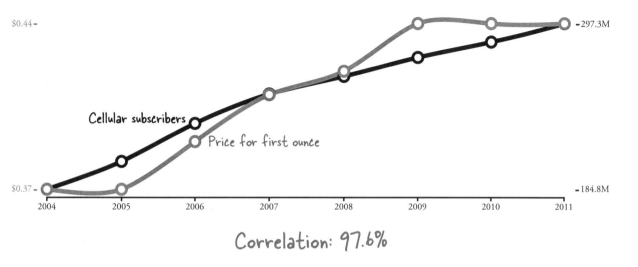

$0.44 -

$0.37 -

Cellular subscribers

Price for first ounce

2004 2005 2006 2007 2008 2009 2010 2011

-297.3M

-184.8M

Correlation: 97.6%

Although the USPS delivers to over 140 million locations, in 2003 the number of possible destinations for a text message overtook the number of possible destinations for a letter.

SOURCES:
Statistic Brain, "Mobile Cellular Subscribers"
U.S. Postal Service

I'm writing an article for Morningstar: Short the NYSE composite and watch a lot of *Two and a Half Men*.

Two and a Half Men's ranking against other CBS shows

vs.

The New York Stock Exchange

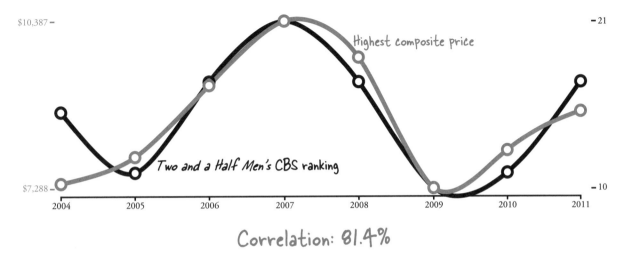

$10,387 —

$7,288 —

— 21

— 10

Highest composite price

Two and a Half Men's CBS ranking

2004   2005   2006   2007   2008   2009   2010   2011

Correlation: 81.4%

Most decisions about buying or selling stocks are currently made and executed by computers. A number of these algorithms are currently working on much weaker correlations than this one. After this book is published, someone will probably write an algorithm to buy and sell stocks based on the popularity of *Two and a Half Men*.

SOURCES:
Wikipedia: "*Two and a Half Men*"
Yahoo! Finance, Historic Market Data: NYSE Composite yearly best
Bloomberg *Businessweek*, "How the Robots Lost: High-Frequency Trading's Rise and Fall"

Sauron's secret weapon: mosquitoes.

Box office gross of Oscar Best Picture winner

vs.

West Nile virus cases in the United States

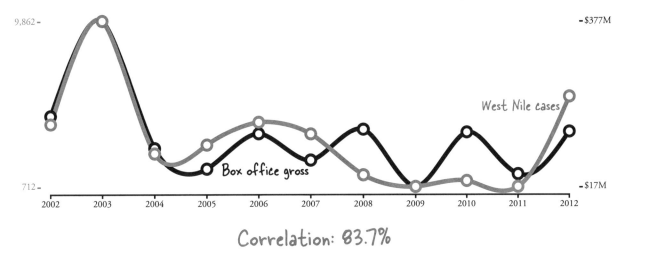

9,862 –

– $377M

West Nile cases

712 –

Box office gross

– $17M

2002 2003 2004 2005 2006 2007 2008 2009 2010 2011 2012

Correlation: 83.7%

The biggest spike was the release of *The Lord of the Rings: The Return of the King*, which coincided with the 2003 West Nile virus outbreak.

SOURCES:
Box Office Mojo, Annual Academy Awards
Centers for Disease Control & Prevention, West Nile virus

Abstinence for employment!

High school sex

vs.

Unemployment

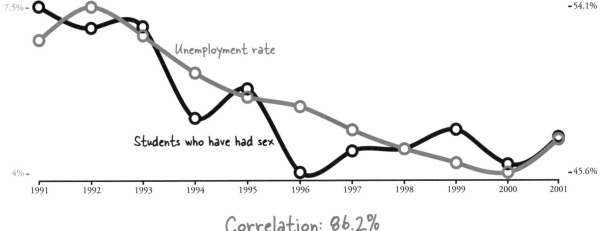

7.5% —

Unemployment rate

— 54.1%

Students who have had sex

4% —

1991 1992 1993 1994 1995 1996 1997 1998 1999 2000 2001

— 45.6%

Correlation: 86.2%

Adding the percentages of high schoolers who use various forms of recognized birth control and the percentage of sexually active high schoolers who report using no form of birth control falls short of 100 percent. At least 5 percent of sexually active high school students are using some newfangled form of birth control *yet unknown* to the CDC.

Sources:
Centers for Disease Control & Prevention
U.S. Bureau of Labor Statistics

Movers, Shakers, Moneymakers

Most cruise liners double as pirate ships when they are not carrying passengers. And sometimes when they are.

Worldwide cruise industry revenue

vs.

Pirate attacks in Indonesia

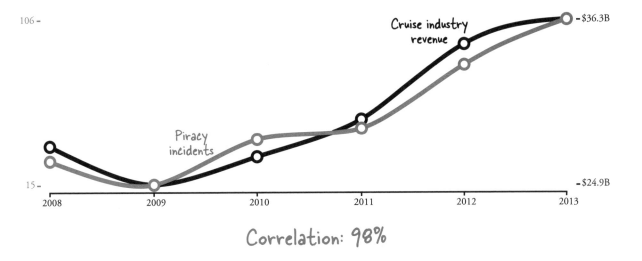

Correlation: 98%

Continued high piracy rates in Indonesia are partly attributable to international bureaucratic red tape. Indonesia has no jurisdiction outside of its own waters, so pirates can evade capture by sailing over toward the sea surrounding Singapore or Malaysia.

SOURCES:
Cruise Market Watch, "2014 Cruise Trends Forecast"
ICC International Maritime Bureau, "Piracy and armed robbery against ships"

Was this a surprise?

Price per gallon of gas

vs.

Lawyers in Texas

82,607 –

Texan lawyers

Average price per gallon

50,212 –

– $3.62

– $1.03

| 92 | 93 | 94 | 95 | 96 | 97 | 98 | 99 | 00 | 01 | 02 | 03 | 04 | 05 | 60 | 70 | 80 | 90 | 00 | 10 | 20 | 03 |

Correlation: 94.4%

Gas prices are highly dependent on where you live. In the United States, a rule of thumb is that Mississippi is roughly the center of a bull's-eye where gas is the cheapest, and gas gets more expensive in rings as you go farther out. California, Oregon, and Washington State are the priciest. Virginia is the exception on the East Coast, with drastically lower gas prices than its neighbors.

SOURCES:
U.S. Energy Information Administration
American Bar Association, National Lawyer Population by State

Smoke a cigarette, one thing leads to another,
and suddenly you have a $15 million bra.

Value of the Victoria's Secret Fantasy Bra

vs.

U.K. men who smoke cigarettes

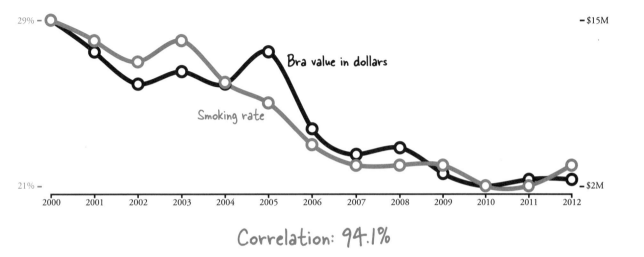

Bra value in dollars

Smoking rate

29% –
21% –

– $15M
– $2M

2000 2001 2002 2003 2004 2005 2006 2007 2008 2009 2010 2011 2012

Correlation: 94.1%

The $15 million bra was called "Red Hot Fantasy" and was modeled by Gisele Bündchen. In 1996, the bra was called the "Million Dollar Miracle." Any guesses what its estimated value was?

SOURCES:
Wikipedia: "Victoria's Secret Fashion Show"
U.K. Office for National Statistics, General Lifestyle Survey and Opinions and Lifestyle Survey

Beer always makes basketball better.

March Madness TV ad revenue

vs.

Breweries in the United States

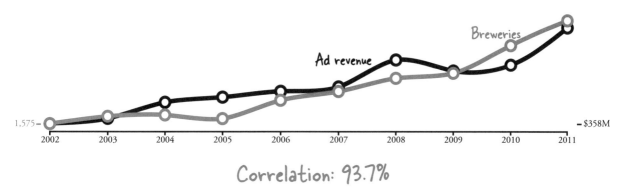

2,751—   —$1.1B

Ad revenue   Breweries

1,575—   —$358M

2002   2003   2004   2005   2006   2007   2008   2009   2010   2011

Correlation: 93.7%

A graph depicting the number of breweries in the United States over the past two hundred years takes on a unique shape. The overall count of breweries is only just now reaching the level it was at in the 1880s. In between was the mid-twentieth-century lull, which had even more of a long-term impact than Prohibition.

SOURCES:

Kantar Media (Remember when we discussed Y-axes in the introduction? Check out how powerful changing the axes on a graph can be by comparing this March Madness line to the one on page 107.)

Beer Institute, Historical Sources

Brewing Industry Research Program

You might want to rethink that pharmaceutical stocking stuffer.

Spending on Christmas gifts

vs.

Juvenile drug arrests

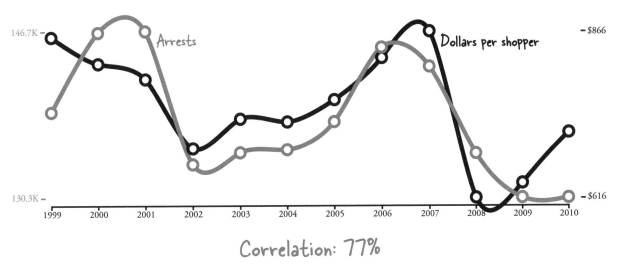

Correlation: 77%

When polled in November 2014, fewer than 10 percent of Americans were willing to report being "not sure" exactly how much they were going to spend on Christmas presents. Everyone else had apparently predicted to the dollar how much they were going to spend.

SOURCES:

Gallup Poll, survey question: "Roughly how much money do you think you personally will spend on Christmas gifts this year?" (1,028 respondents, at least 50 percent of whom were cell phone respondents contacted by using random digit dialing methods. Hats off to those who respond to survey cold calls on their cell phone.)

U.S. Department of Justice, Federal Bureau of Investigation: Uniform Crime Reports

SpaceX reveals its secret spaceship building material.

LEGO revenue

vs.

Worldwide revenue from commercial space launches

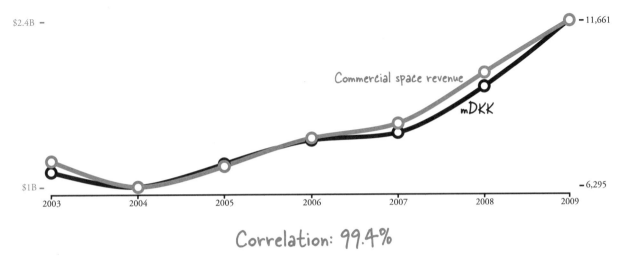

$2.4B —

Commercial space revenue

mDKK

$1B —

2003   2004   2005   2006   2007   2008   2009

— 11,661

— 6,295

Correlation: 99.4%

If you're paying close attention to the graphs, you may be wondering what "mDKK" is. The answer would be "millions of Danish krones." LEGO Group is based in Denmark, so all of its finances are in the Danish krone. The krone has a terrible exchange rate to the USD.

SOURCES:
LEGO Group Annual Reports
Federal Aviation Administration, "Commercial Space Transportation: 2010 Year in Review"

Domino's is a front company: The real reason they have pizza is to feed their army of computer hackers.

Earnings per share of Domino's Pizza Group

vs.

Economic loss due to cybercrime

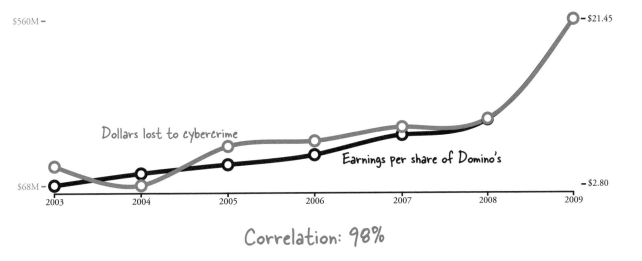

$560M –   ○ – $21.45

Dollars lost to cybercrime

$68M –   – $2.80
    2003   2004   2005   2006   2007   2008   2009

Earnings per share of Domino's

Correlation: 98%

"Cybercrime" is incredibly difficult to track. Besides the surface difficulty of defining cybercrime and tracking cause of losses, many local police departments are simply not equipped to handle cybercrime reports.

SOURCES:
Domino's Pizza Annual Reports
Internet Crime Complaint Center, referred cases only

All-natural eyeliner.

Cosmopolitan magazine ad revenue

vs.

Coal imports to Germany

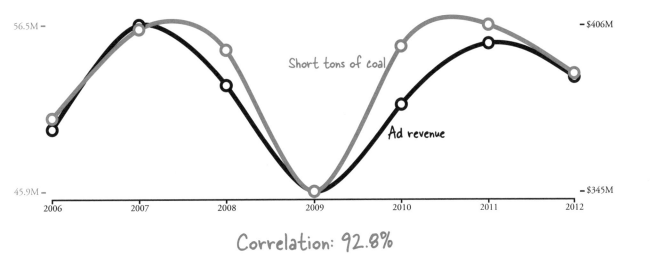

56.5M –

45.9M –

Short tons of coal

Ad revenue

– $406M

– $345M

2006   2007   2008   2009   2010   2011   2012

Correlation: 92.8%

Cosmopolitian is one of the top money-making magazines. However, it doesn't even begin to compare to *People*, which brought in nearly $1 billion in 2012.

SOURCES:
The Association of Magazine Media
U.S. Energy Information Administration, International Energy Statistics

A Krispy Kreme diet doesn't work with a compact car.

Krispy Kreme doughnut stores

vs.

Market share for midsize vans

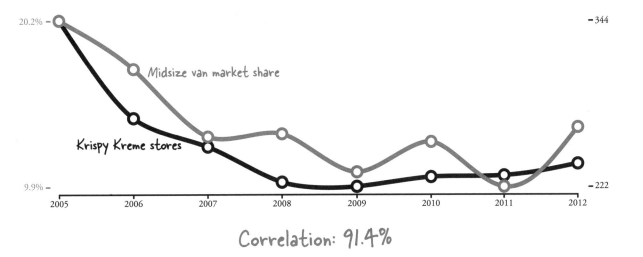

20.2% —

Midsize van market share

Krispy Kreme stores

9.9% —

2005   2006   2007   2008   2009   2010   2011   2012

— 344

— 222

Correlation: 91.4%

Krispy Kreme is incredibly interested in being a deluxe brand. Since 2005, they have closed hundreds of locations housed in gas stations and grocery stores that made them look cheap and "normal."

SOURCES:
Advertising Age, "Krispy Kreme's Secret Growth Recipe"
U.S. Department of Transportation, Bureau of Transportation Statistics

Halo is a documentary dropped off by aliens.

Physical retail sales of video games

vs.

UFO sightings in Massachusetts

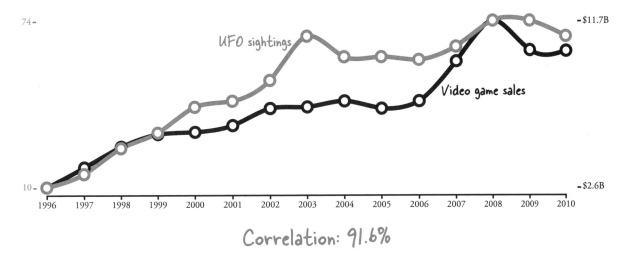

UFO sightings

Video game sales

Correlation: 91.6%

Physical sales of video games hit their all-time peak in 2008. As in, they will never, ever be that high again. Annual sales have since halved as the internet becomes the go-to distribution method.

SOURCES:
Entertainment Software Association, "Essential Facts About the Computer and Video Game Industry" (2014)
National UFO Reporting Center

Because nothing wears out your shoes like someone else hiking up Mount Everest.

Shoe sales

vs.

Mount Everest ascents

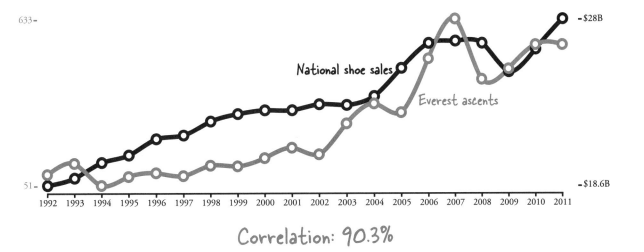

633–   –$28B

National shoe sales

Everest ascents

51–   –$18.6B

1992 1993 1994 1995 1996 1997 1998 1999 2000 2001 2002 2003 2004 2005 2006 2007 2008 2009 2010 2011

Correlation: 90.3%

Contrary to popular belief, exposure to the cold and frostbite are not the top killers on Everest—they only account for about 12 percent of fatalities. One-third of deaths are due to something much simpler and predictable at five and a half miles up: falling.

SOURCES:
U.S. Department of Commerce, Monthly Retail Trade Report
CBC News, "Mount Everest by the numbers" (Ascents tracked by Eberhard Jurgalski for www.8000ers.com.)

Social networking is turning us into windbags.

Facebook users

vs.

Total U.S. wind power generation capacity

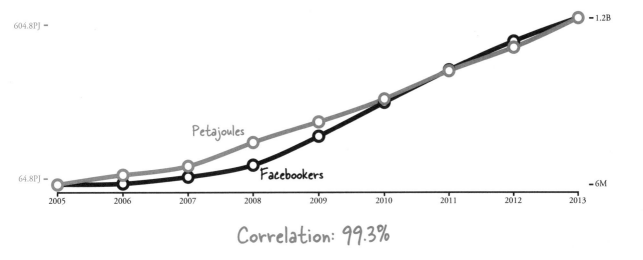

604.8PJ –

64.8PJ –

Petajoules

Facebookers

– 1.2B

– 6M

2005 2006 2007 2008 2009 2010 2011 2012 2013

Correlation: 99.3%

In order to time travel in *Back to the Future*, Dr. Brown needed 1.21 gigawatts of electricity. He got it from nuclear power, and later lightning, which is good, because at a measly 1.5MW maximum generating capacity and 25 percent average output, it would take more than 3,000 wind turbines to send the DeLorean anywhere interesting.

SOURCES:

The Guardian: Datablog, "Facebook: 10 years of social networking, in numbers"

U.S. Energy Information Administration (A petajoule is one quadrillion joules. Joules are a unit of energy, which makes them a more logical choice than the utility standard "kilowatt-hours." Since kilowatts are a unit of energy over time, measuring kilowatt-hours instead of megajoules is like measuring distance in miles-per-hour-hours instead of just miles.)

Nothin' is sexier than a Harley.

Harley-Davidson's motorcycle revenue

vs.

U.S. fertility rate

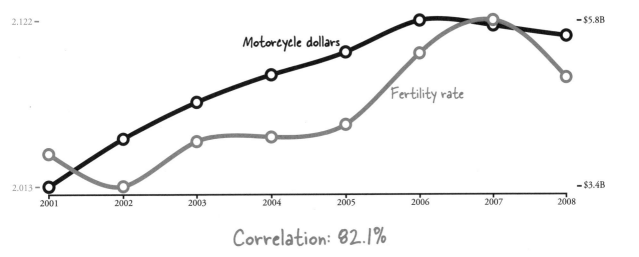

Correlation: 82.1%

Any fertility rate below 2,110 (2.11 children per woman) results in a net loss of population based on average mortality. Without immigration, the U.S. population would decline.

SOURCES:
Harley-Davidson's Annual Reports
U.S. National Center for Health Statistics, National Vital Statistics Report

Germany has been selling us flying cigars that look like cars.

German passenger car sales in the United States

vs.

Reports of UFOs that look like cigars

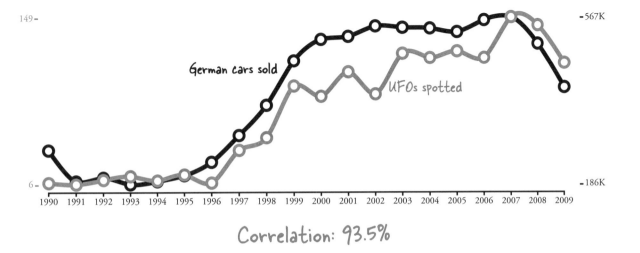

149 —

German cars sold

UFOs spotted

— 567K

6 —

— 186K

1990 1991 1992 1993 1994 1995 1996 1997 1998 1999 2000 2001 2002 2003 2004 2005 2006 2007 2008 2009

Correlation: 93.5%

The jump in UFO reports in the late nineties is due not to an actual increase in UFO sightings, but more likely to a change in the ease of reporting: the internet. Once you no longer have to call a phone number and talk to a real person to report what you see, the likelihood that you'll be willing to file a report dramatically increases.

SOURCES:
U.S. Bureau of Transportation Statistics, National Transportation Statistics
National UFO Reporting Center

Forget health care—I'm moving to Canada
because postal rates are too damn high!

Cost to send a postcard via USPS

vs.

Population of Canada

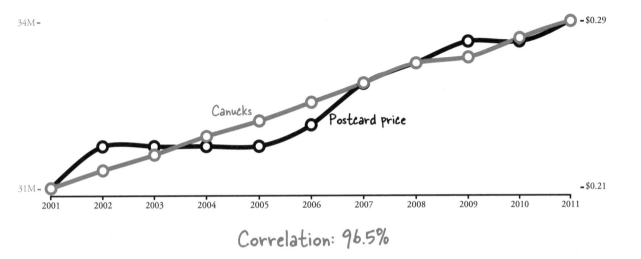

34M –
31M –

Canucks

Postcard price

2001 2002 2003 2004 2005 2006 2007 2008 2009 2010 2011

– $0.29
– $0.21

Correlation: 96.5%

This is actually a really poor reason to move to Canada. Not because postal rates are a bad reason to make a life decision. Rather, in Canada, there's no special postal rate for postcards. A postcard would cost nearly three times as much to mail in Canada as in the United States.

SOURCES:
U.S. Postal Service, "United States Domestic Postage Rate: Recent History" and unpublished data
Statistics Canada, "Population by year, by province and territory"
Canada Post, "Postage Stamps"

Money doesn't grow on trees, unless that money is for bingo and those trees are houseplants.

Estimated revenue from all bingo games

vs.

Homes with indoor houseplants

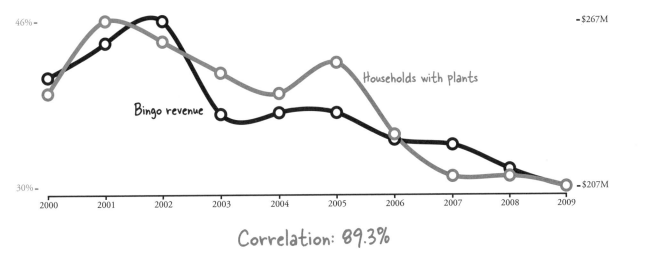

46% -   - $267M

Bingo revenue

Households with plants

30% -   - $207M

2000 2001 2002 2003 2004 2005 2006 2007 2008 2009

Correlation: 89.3%

I like to imagine that instead of using a survey, the National Gardening Association sneaks into every house in the sample set to check for plants.

SOURCES:
Christiansen Capital Advisors LLC, "Gaming Revenue by Industry," prepared for the American Gaming Association
The National Gardening Association, National Gardening Survey (2,000 respondents)

Pandora's new business model reportedly involves encouraging the Yankees to recruit players from high schools.

Pandora's net loss in millions

vs.

Average age of New York Yankees batters

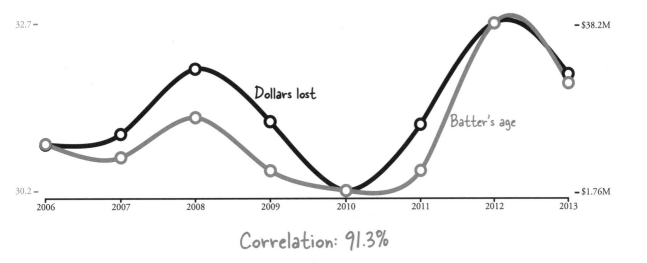

Correlation: 91.3%

Pandora now pays enough in royalties every year to give $1 to every man, woman, and child in the United States. Even though Pandora has a premium version subscribers can pay for (Pandora One), they still make around seven times as much on advertising on the free accounts as they do from the paid accounts.

SOURCES:
Pandora's SEC Filings
Baseball-Reference.com, New York Yankees Team Yearly Batting Stats

Conspiracy theory: Bill Gates controls congress.

Microsoft's revenue

vs.

Political action committees

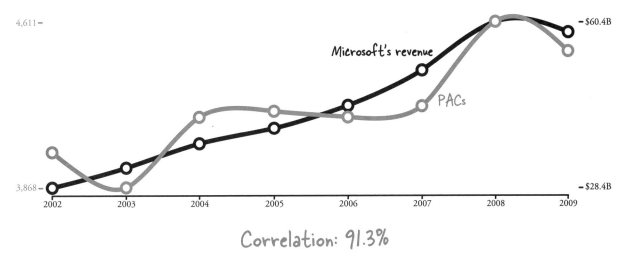

4,611 —

Microsoft's revenue

PACs

— $60.4B

3,868 —   — $28.4B

| 2002 | 2003 | 2004 | 2005 | 2006 | 2007 | 2008 | 2009 |

Correlation: 91.3%

In 2012, an estimated $2.6 billion was spent on influencing the presidential election. This would have been enough money to produce another thousand episodes of *The West Wing*.

SOURCES:
Microsoft Investor Relations, Earnings Releases 2002–2009
U.S. Federal Election Commission, Press Release, May 2009
Entertainment Weekly, "The Lowe Down" (2002)

Oh, the places you'll go, with oil in tow!

Aggregate worldwide income of oil companies

vs.

Travel books published

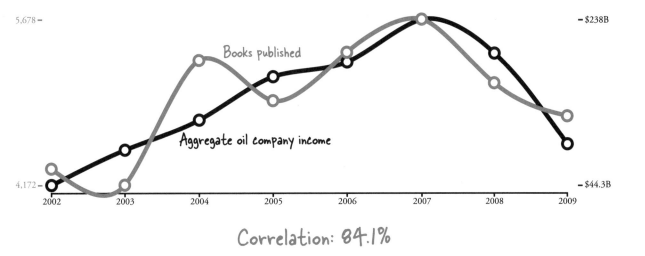

5,678 —

Books published

Aggregate oil company income

4,172 —

2002   2003   2004   2005   2006   2007   2008   2009

— $238B

— $44.3B

Correlation: 84.1%

Of the companies in the world with the highest revenue, the only one in the top five that isn't an oil company is Walmart.

Sources:
Carl H. Pforzheimer & Co., New York, NY, Comparative Oil Company Statements
Bowker, New Book Titles and Editions

Famous Folks

Bruce Willis is the hard-boiled type.

Bruce Willis film appearances

vs.

People killed by an exploding boiler

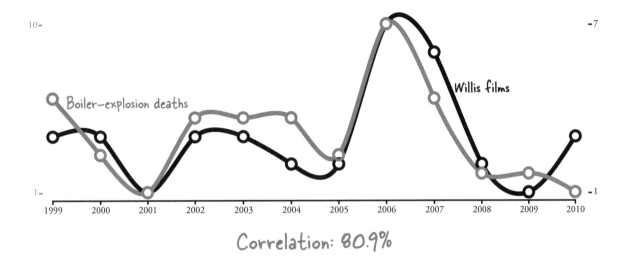

Boiler-explosion deaths

Willis films

Correlation: 80.9%

2006 is the year Bruce Willis appeared in the most un-Bruce-Willis-like films. His credits that year include such action thrillers as *Fast Food Nation* and the voice of RJ, a cartoon raccoon in *Over the Hedge*.

SOURCES:
Internet Movie Database: Bruce Willis
Centers for Disease Control & Prevention, Detailed Mortality Data

Rachel Weisz's next blockbuster is so hot,
it will melt your pajamas.

Rachel Weisz film appearances

vs.

Deaths caused by exposure to melting pajamas

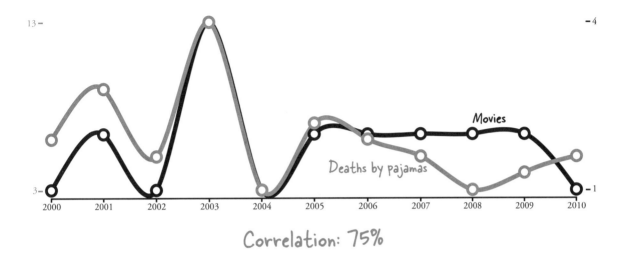

Correlation: 75%

Significantly more women are killed by melting pajamas than men. Here, "significantly" means upwards of 300 percent. (Admittedly, this is only a disparity of 3 to 5 people per year.)

SOURCES:

Internet Movie Database: Rachel Weisz (You caught me; I'm counting the release of the deleted scenes from *About a Boy* to make that jump to four films in 2003. I feel safe admitting that down here in the footnote.)

Centers for Disease Control & Prevention, Detailed Mortality Data

Either "accidental" or "just finished *Gigli*."

Ben Affleck film appearances

vs.

Accidental poisonings by pesticides

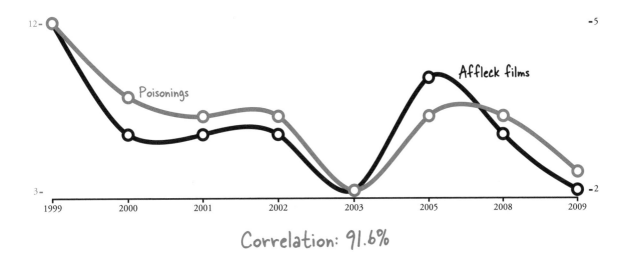

12 - (1999)
3 -
1999   2000   2001   2002   2003   2005   2008   2009

- 5
- 2

Poisonings

Affleck films

Correlation: 91.6%

Ben Affleck's full name is Benjamin Géza Affleck-Boldt. I, for one, would like to see him credited just once as "Benjamin Boldt," if only to confuse viewers.

SOURCES:
Internet Movie Database: Ben Affleck
Centers for Disease Control & Prevention, Detailed Mortality Data

The NBA should investigate.

Points scored by Kobe Bryant

vs.

U.K. citizens who immigrated to the United States

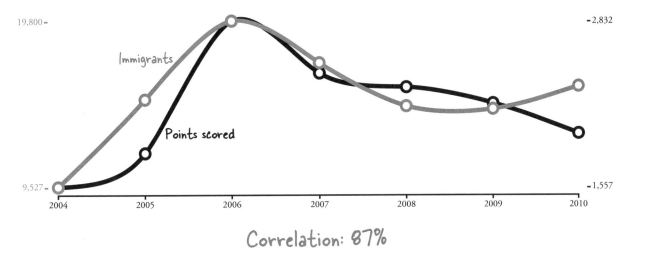

19,800 –
Immigrants
Points scored
9,527 –
2004   2005   2006   2007   2008   2009   2010

– 2,832

– 1,557

Correlation: 87%

No word yet on whether U.K.-to-U.S. immigration is affecting tea consumption rates in the United States.

SOURCES:
National Basketball Association, Players: Kobe Bryant
Department of Homeland Security

Morgan Freeman takes to narrating nose surgeries.

Morgan Freeman film appearances

vs.

Women who received cosmetic nose surgery

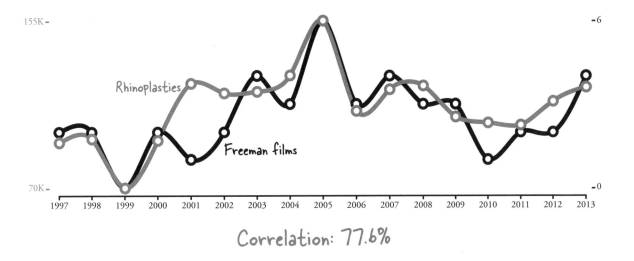

155K -   - 6

Rhinoplasties

Freeman films

70K -   - 0

1997 1998 1999 2000 2001 2002 2003 2004 2005 2006 2007 2008 2009 2010 2011 2012 2013

Correlation: 77.6%

The "Morgan Freeman Effect" describes situations where one feature of something, like an actor's soothing voice, makes up for everything else, like a terrible plotline. At least, according to whoever wrote the Urban Dictionary entry about it. I've never actually heard anyone say "Morgan Freeman Effect" in real life.

SOURCES:
Internet Movie Database: Morgan Freeman
The American Society for Aesthetic Plastic Surgery, cosmetic surgery statistics
Urban Dictionary

One of the many reasons Jennifer Lawrence
should appear in more films.

Jennifer Lawrence film appearances

vs.

GDP of Australia

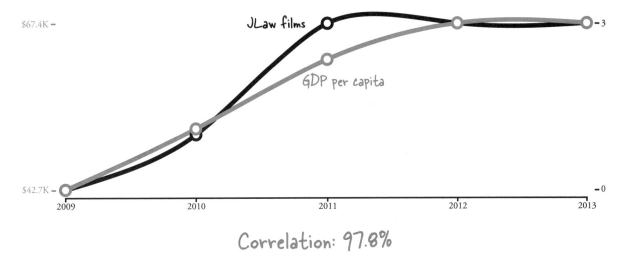

$67.4K –

$42.7K –

2009   2010   2011   2012   2013

JLaw films

GDP per capita

– 3

– 0

Correlation: 97.8%

Wool is a big contributor to the Australian GDP. The majority of Australia's wool exports, more than $1 billion worth of wool annually, goes directly to China.

Sources:
Wikipedia: "Jennifer Lawrence"
The World Bank, GDP per capita—current USD
Government of Australia, Australia's Top 25 Exports, Goods & Services (This isn't a citation to an article about the Government of Australia, it's a citation directly to "The government of Australia." They stand behind their statistics down there.)

I hear Natalie Portman's agent is pitching
a *Star Wars* Holiday Spectacular.

Natalie Portman film appearances

vs.

Real Christmas trees sold in the United States

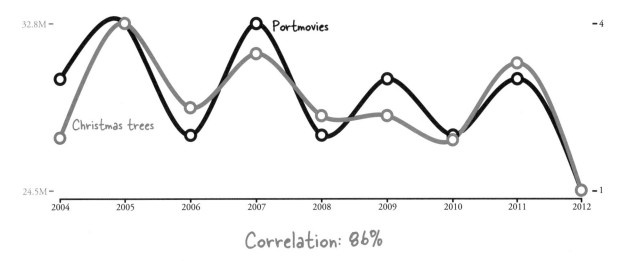

Correlation: 86%

The data also shows that Americans strongly prefer real Christmas trees to fake trees at a rate of more than 2:1. However, this may be a case of organizational bias. The source of that data is "realchristmastrees.org."

SOURCES:
Internet Movie Database: Natalie Portman
National Christmas Tree Association, Consumer Survey (The NCTA does not report how many people they surveyed to obtain these estimates.)

Nic Cage never said, "Don't try this at home" before jumping off the aircraft carrier in *National Treasure*.

Nicolas Cage film appearances

vs.

Number of people who drowned by falling into a swimming pool

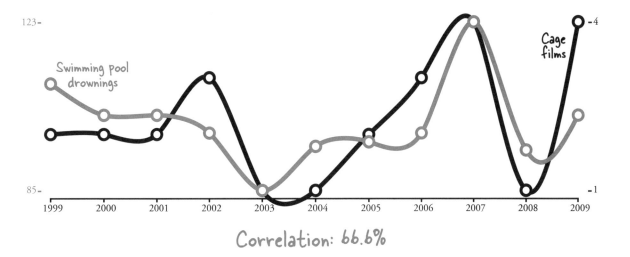

123-

Swimming pool
drownings

-4

Cage
films

85-

-1

1999 2000 2001 2002 2003 2004 2005 2006 2007 2008 2009

Correlation: 66.6%

Swimming pool drowning rates also seasonally correlate with frozen yogurt consumption. They both go up in the summer and down in the winter. You might say, "It's warm outside," but I say it's a conspiracy!

SOURCES:
Internet Movie Database: Nicolas Cage
Centers for Disease Control & Prevention, Detailed Mortality Data

Please put your tray table up, and the football in your teammate's possession!

Passing attempts by NFL quarterback Drew Brees

vs.

Complaints filed against airlines in the United States

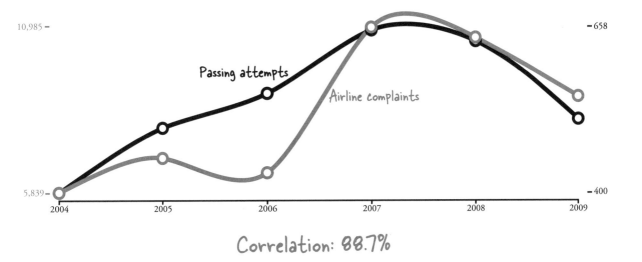

New Orleans Saints passing attempts
correlates with
Airline complaints

Correlation: 88.7%

Your chances of winning the Powerball from one ticket are around 1 in 175 million. Your odds of dying on any single commercial airline flight are closer to 1 in 10 million. Thus, it makes more statistical sense to attempt suicide by flying on a commercial airline than to get rich by buying a lottery ticket.

SOURCES:
National Football League, New Orleans Saints
U.S. Department of Transportation, Aviation Consumer Protection Division, Air Travel Consumer Report
The Huffington Post, "A Statistician's View: What Are Your Chances of Winning the Powerball Lottery?"

Casting Chris Evans as Captain America
was a truly earth-shattering choice.

Chris Evans film appearances

vs.

Magnitude 8+ earthquakes

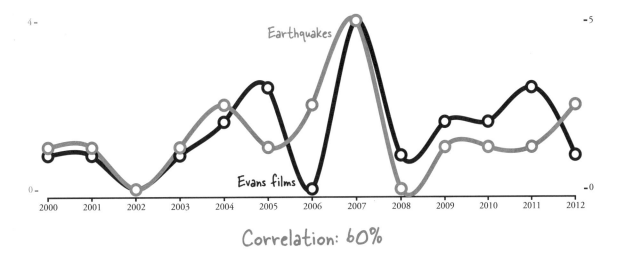

Earthquakes

Evans films

Correlation: 60%

The USGS now tracks nearly twenty thousand earthquakes per year. Magnitude 8+ earthquakes, however, are only expected to occur at a frequency of around once per year. The increased frequency since 2004 is attributable to random chance—it's spurious.

SOURCES:
Wikipedia: "Chris Evans (actor)"
U.S. Geological Survey, Magnitude 8.0–9.9 Earthquakes Worldwide

Lionel Messi is *Captain Argentina*. It's the same as *Captain America* but with less spandex.

Goals scored by Lionel Messi for Argentina

vs.

Top-grossing Marvel movie

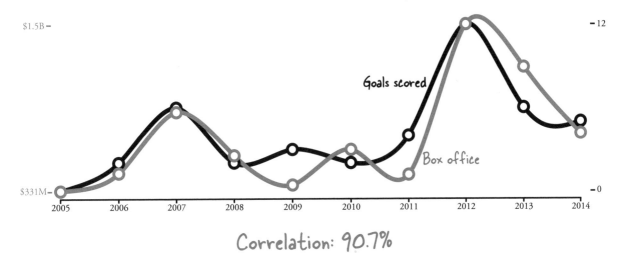

$1.5B —

$331M —

2005 2006 2007 2008 2009 2010 2011 2012 2013 2014

Goals scored

Box office

— 12

— 0

Correlation: 90.7%

The 2012 Marvel box office spike was *The Avengers*—which was also the first Marvel movie produced by Disney.

Sources:
Wikipedia: "Lionel Messi"
Box Office Mojo, Franchises: Marvel Comics

The patent office now hires clerks in lockstep with Indiana Jones sequels.

Harrison Ford film appearances

vs.

Patents issued by the United States Patent and Trademark Office

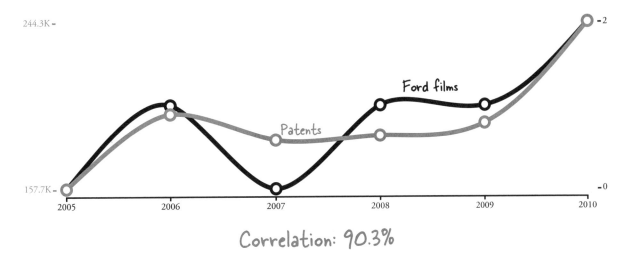

Correlation: 90.3%

IBM alone accounted for more than 5,800 of the patents issued in 2010. In 2013, IBM was issued 6,788 patents. That's more than 18 patents *every single day*.

SOURCES:
Internet Movie Database: Harrison Ford
U.S. Patent and Trademark Office

Coming this summer: Liam Neeson shops at Walmart.

Liam Neeson film appearances

vs.

Walmart sales

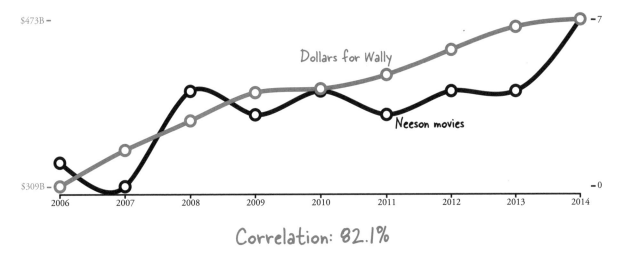

Correlation: 82.1%

If the parking lots of every Walmart were put in one place, they would cover an area three times the size of Manhattan.

SOURCES:
Internet Movie Database: Liam Neeson
Walmart Annual Reports
Wal-Mart Watch, "It's Not Easy Being Green: The Truth about Wal-Mart's Environmental Makeover."

Crocodile attacks in Cleveland: 0.

Field goals made by LeBron James

vs.

High-profile crocodile attacks in Southeast Asia and Australia

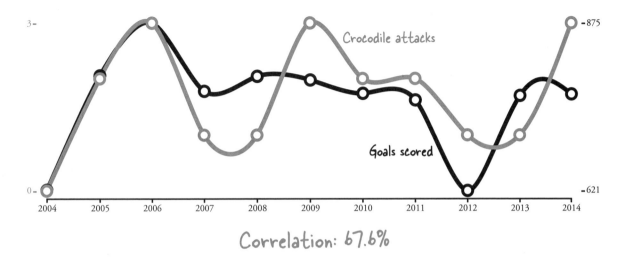

Crocodile attacks

Goals scored

Correlation: 67.6%

These numbers are based on only the most notable attacks, as arbitrarily determined by users of Wikipedia. The Nile crocodile is responsible for hundreds more attacks in areas with less reliable reporting and recording systems in place.

SOURCES:
Basketball-Reference.com: LeBron James
Wikipedia: "Crocodile attack"

Keira has the most outrageous contract rider ever:
10 million pounds of king crab.

Keira Knightley film appearances

vs.

Total supply of king crab in the United States

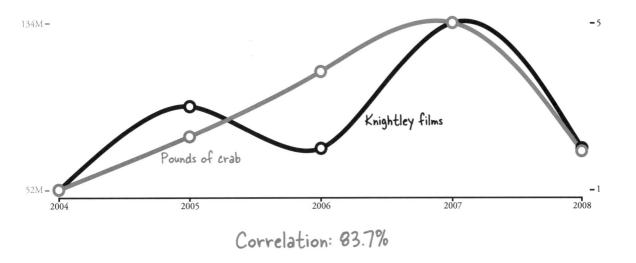

134M –

52M –

2004   2005   2006   2007   2008

– 5

– 1

Knightley films

Pounds of crab

Correlation: 83.7%

The king crab fishing industry peaked in 1980. By the time Keira was born five years later, overfishing caused the industry to decline by 90 percent.

SOURCES:
Internet Movie Database: Keira Knightley
U.S. National Oceanic and Atmospheric Administration, National Marine Fisheries Service, Fisheries of the United States

About the Author

Tyler Vigen is a student at Harvard Law School. He created the Spurious Correlations website during a week before finals, when he probably should have been studying. Prior to attending Harvard, Tyler was trained in visual intelligence collection and analysis by the military.